New and Collected Poems: 1975–2015

Other Books by Jay Parini

POETRY

Singing in Time (1972)
Anthracite Country (1982)
Town Life (1988)
House of Days (1997)
The Art of Subtraction: New and Selected Poems (2005)

FICTION

The Love Run (1980)
The Patch Boys (1986)
The Last Station (1990)
Bay of Arrows (1992)
Benjamin's Crossing (1997)
The Apprentice Lover (2002)
The Passages of H.M. (2010)

NONFICTION

Theodore Roethke: An American Romantic (1979)
An Invitation to Poetry (1987)
John Steinbeck: A Biography (2004)
Some Necessary Angels: Essays on Literature and Politics (1997)
Robert Frost: A Life (1999)
One Matchless Time: A Life of William Faulkner (2004)
The Art of Teaching (2005)
Why Poetry Matters (2008)
Promised Land: Thirteen Books That Changed America (2008)
Jesus: The Human Face of God (2013)
Empire of Self: A Life of Gore Vidal (2015)

New and Collected Poems: 1975–2015

Jay Parini

BEACON PRESS
BOSTON

Beacon Press
Boston, Massachusetts
www.beacon.org

Beacon Press books
are published under the auspices of
the Unitarian Universalist Association of Congregations.

19 18 17 16   8 7 6 5 4 3 2 1

This book is printed on acid-free paper that meets the uncoated paper ANSI/
NISO specifications for permanence as revised in 1992.

Text design by Ruth Maassen

Library of Congress Cataloging-in-Publication Data

Parini, Jay.
  [Poems. Selections]
  New and collected poems: 1975-2015 / Jay Parini.
     pages ; cm
  ISBN 978-0-8070-3013-4 (hardcover : alk. paper) —
  ISBN 978-0-8070-3014-1 (ebook)
  I. Title.
  PS3566.A65A6 2016
  811'.54—dc23
                        2015025759

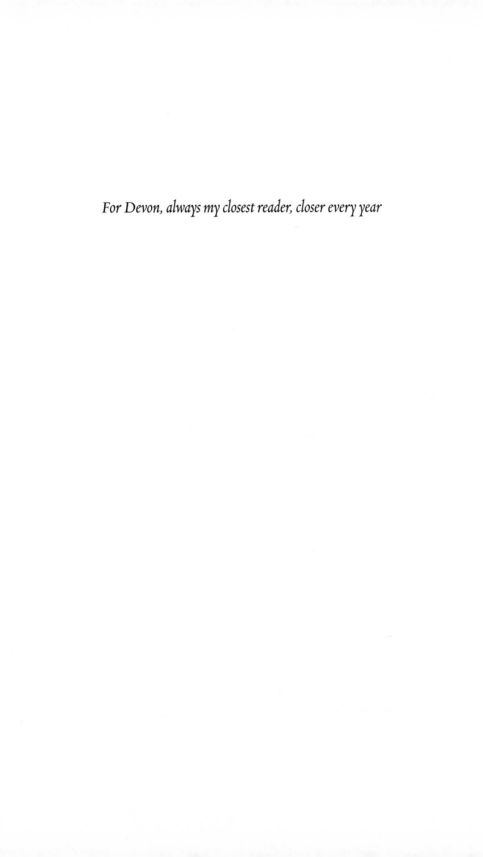

For Devon, always my closest reader, closer every year

CONTENTS

from TOWN LIFE (1983–1988)

from ANTHRACITE COUNTRY (1975–1982)

AUTHOR'S NOTE

This book contains most of the poems written in the past forty years that I wish to stand by. It begins with a volume of new poems —those written in the past decade—called *West Mountain Epilogue*. Most of the poems from *The Art of Subtraction* (2005), *House of Days* (1998), *Town Life* (1988), and *Anthracite Country* (1982) are here as well, though I have excluded *Singing in Time* (1972), my first volume, published in Scotland when I was a graduate student. In a few instances, with the poems previously published in volume form, I have changed a word or phrase, added a line, altered punctuation slightly, or, in two instances, altered a title.

I would like to thank the editors of the following publications, where some of these poems first appeared: *Agni*, *The American Scholar*, *The Atlantic*, *Boston Review*, *Chicago Review*, *The Dark Horse*, *The Florida Review*, *The Georgia Review*, *Graham House Review*, *Harper's*, *The Hudson Review*, *The Iowa Review*, *The Kenyon Review*, *Lowestoft Chronicle*, *Michigan Quarterly Review*, *Miramar*, *The Missouri Review*, *Ontario Review*, *Oxford Poetry*, *The New Yorker*, *The Paris Review*, *Partisan Review*, *Poetry*, *PN Review*, *Plume*, *The New Republic*, *Sewanee Review*, *The Southern Review*, *Scottish International*, *Smartish Pace*, *South Atlantic Quarterly*, *Tar River Poetry*, *Verse*, *The Virginia Quarterly Review*, *The Yale Review*.

New Poems:
West Mountain Epilogue

(2006–2015)

The Language of Mines

Spring Snow

Spring snow is falling on the Lackawanna:
flakes like butterflies that fail to land.
The river is a thick black tongue tonight,
wet-leathery and dumb.
I listen like a fool
to what cannot or won't be said.
I'm old or young, I can't quite tell.
This bygone winter was a kind of hell,
but now it's over. I can dream
of daffodils like women in their yellow dresses.
I would love to suck their long green stems
and twirl a finger in their tresses.
Just below me, I can feel
the trembling roots and tubers,
suck and cipher in the sudden swell.
And something in the air's alive again.
The ice-floes shelve and break
along the shoreline's smudge of pain.
I lean into the shadows, come what may.
Even the stones melt fast around me
as the ground gives way.

Over the River

My grandmother in northeast Pennsylvania
on her tiny farm beside the river
fed her chickens every day at dawn.
I used to watch her scattering the grain
like John D. Rockefeller scattered dimes.
She was very poor and wanted nothing,
with the rising loaves in her fat kitchen.
Everyone who came there fed to fullness.
I was just a child but like a prince
I drank raw milk in chalices of glass
and wore a crown of many feathers
that she plucked before she cooked the goose.
On her porch, in sandals of bare skin,
she chatted with the sparrows in her eaves
while August sun spread gold doubloons
upon the purling Susquehanna River,
which of course she didn't need to own.

West Mountain Epilogue

All day the soot-rain fell and slantwise,
coal dust pouring through a purple scrim
above the city in its August steam,
its redbrick buildings with their broken teeth
and warehouse wings,
white plastic trash beside the sidewalks,
ghost-bags lifted into swirls
as trains dragged slowly through the center,
axles turning in the roundhouse,
in the weedy rail yard where the rooftops
hummed in drizzle like a silent migraine
in the damp hot drowse.

I was in my room, not in my room
but talking back to talk inside my head
in passing phrases,
reading to myself and writing to myself.

Go! said the blue jay. *Go now. Go!*

And so I walked toward West Mountain, miles away.
I climbed throughout that afternoon
in rain that wept my eyes and cooled my forehead.

Climbed on slippery gray stones,
on weed-skim, shelves of slate, black moss
beside a creek that foamed and gargled
as the banks spilled over.

I was on all fours
and clambering through alder-damp,

through vetch, feeling my way
toward a lookout near the first high peak,
where someone told me Indians had graves
and white men, too.

                        I half-believed
in all-souls clashing, found
red jasper arrowheads beside the creek
but didn't keep them, didn't want to think
about that fury, the unburied past.

The city lay behind me under mist,
a cindery gray spread.
I couldn't see it from the ledge when I looked back.
But don't look back, I said, keep saying,
as the long goodbye goes on and on.

I made it to the other side that day:
walked, crawled, and slid—a snail at times
on my slim ass, my pearly sled. And found my footing
on a slow descent toward the edge of it,
a further ripple in the westward ho,
as I kept walking, sometimes
hacking my way through
a tangle of old-growth,
day after day. And once I paused
beside a burning bush of sunlight,
where a voice said *yes I am.*

And then a rainbow spread before me,
and I heard the feet of many pilgrims,
and knew I'd left that Lackawanna light

forever and for good. I knew I'd walk
into the wilderness of dark green mountains,
settle into soft leaves, mulch, moraine,
then sleep to wake beside a curling stream
as dawn-light beckoned
by a gusty, wet-black road,
not looking back but not forgetting
where I'd been and how I'd been—
that hard coal city in its carbon steam.

Home

is where the old discarded selves
scurry under floors.
Thinking they are dead,
we imagine exoskeletons all heaped there,
humped and moldering.
But mandibles, a million working jaws,
jostle and survive.

A Knock at Midnight

There must be some error.
Are you sure you have the right address?

I'm not the one you really wanted.
He's probably the one who lives next door,
the one without a door.

In any case I'm younger than you'd think.
I've got young children
and a lovely wife, and she's young, too.

I'm not the man for this great mission.
I detest long journeys.
I have fear of heights and snakes and flying.
And I'm so allergic: everything
is bad for my digestion.

And I don't like corridors or caves.
In open spaces, I am agoraphobic.
Truly, I have not been feeling well.

My heart beats crazily, and wakes my neighbors.
Heroism doesn't ring my bell.

Please, listen to my words!
What do you want with me at this late hour?

His Morning Meditations

My father in this lonely room of prayer
listens at the window
in the little house of his own dreams.

He has come a long way just to listen,
over seas and sorrow, through the narrow gate
of his deliverance.

And he dwells here now,
beyond the valley and the shadow, too,
in silence mustered day by dawn.

It has come to this sweet isolation
in the eye of God, the earliest of mornings
in his chambered skull, this frost of thought.

Snowday in Pittston

The hardest objects fell to white:
old workings, wheels and windlass,
chunks of anthracite like knuckles
in the pails on porches.
The cars lay buried by the curbside.

Trees swept underneath the sheets
of ice and snow.
The hedgerows zigzagged,
mounds of whiteness in the empty yards
as tramlines lost their way to work.

And only in the afternoon of sun
did pathways open, house to house.
Young mothers brushed the sidewalks clean
as fathers in their rank cold oily basements
lifted coal into the hoppers.

Gradually children went outside
to wander in the silent bright-lit wonder
that had brought them this:
a shimmering on surfaces that made them strange,
a blanch of empty and uncounted hours.

A Dream of Stones

I dreamed about the stones
and then I found them
somewhere in my pocket.

Clouds swept by
and cars swept by.
The subway and the carriage,
glass and gold,
went humming through the tube,
the pairs of horses with their heads held high
and Westward Ho!

It was snowing heavily
throughout the day
in Puerto Rico.
It was hot on top
of Everest and every single Alp.
On a stormy afternoon in some dark gulch
the weathermen went home.

O sages, where's the weight of wisdom?
I have walked behind the holy men
and holy women in my whitest gown.
The stones rang elsewhere
and outside the great procession.

In the water once in that green summer
of my skinny knees,
I swam the River Susquehanna

and the stones were everywhere
and smooth and white
along the banks.
                    And afterward
I lay and slobbered on the suede of moss
and must have swallowed
half a dozen stones
like luscious oysters, raw and wet.

Lackawanna Rail

All night the engines slept below us
in their bulky shed,
while boxcars waited,
wagon after wagon filled with coal.
I woke up early, rubbed my eyes,
and watched the rail yard gather to itself
its definitions:
corrugated iron rippling roof,
a red brick wheelhouse centering the lot,
and blue rails streaming north and south.
We'd come out early
on the night before to eat and drink:
cold sandwiches and beer
amid the honeybees that stuck
and fed in blood-bright flowers
as we smoked a pack of Lucky Strikes
and lied about the girls
we loved so well. The night sprayed
stars, and fireflies
temporized in ghost-capped hogweed,
and the crickets thrummed.
We were just fourteen,
both willowy and sad
with all the world before us like a hill
that wouldn't budge.
We slept against its shoulder
through the August night.
I watched you breathing in the brittle grass
with dandelions almost like a crown
of bloom in your blond hair.

In T-shirt, shorts, and yellow sneakers,
you were like a girl
with slender wrists and puffy lips.
Your eyelids trembled,
and I had to wonder what you dreamed.
Whatever we had said,
the night before was nothing now.
I didn't weigh it heavily
in breaking dawn, its bony light
and sickly sweet fermented breeze
that drew across a beer can
spilled nearby. And soon the wagons
clicked and swayed as pistons
cranked the day into a date,
a time when something was accomplished,
hard coal hauled from here to there
as butterflies and birds began
to graze from flower to flower,
from minute into hour,
and everything around us
flushed and fluttered, then broke free.

A Night in the Field

I didn't mean to stay so late
or lie there in the grass
all summer afternoon and thoughtless
as the kite of sun caught in the tree-limbs
and the crimson field began to burn,
then tilt way.
      I hung on
handily as night lit up the sky's black skull
and star-flakes fell as if forever—
fat white petals of a far-off flower
like manna on the plains.

A ripe moon lifted in the east,
its eye so focused,
knowing what I knew but had forgotten
of the only death I'll ever really need
to keep me going.

Did I sleep to wake or wake to sleep?

I slipped in seams through many layers,
soil and subsoil, rooting
in the loamy depths of my creation,
where at last I almost felt at home.

But rose at dawn in rosy light,
beginning in the dew-sop long-haired grass,
having been taken, tossed,
having gone down, a blackened tooth
in sugary old gums, that ground
where innocence is found, unfound,

making my way toward the barn,
its beams alight,
its rafters blazing in the red-ball sun.

Happy Hour

Sam's Bar & Grille, January 1964

It's a busy silence they maintain,
like holy brothers hounding after God.
They've tramped through snow in heavy boots
and will avoid the niceties of talk,
big-shouldered men who married young,
just out of school, as everybody did.
The children came and then they went,
although a few of them have now grown silvery
beside their fathers and their brothers, too.
Today they watch the flaxen sunlight
settle for an hour that means so much
if you've been standing on a warehouse floor
or punching holes or driving forklifts
in a timeless dull fluorescent buzz.
They come here for the bar and not the grille,
to nurse their beers in yellow rows.
Sam knows who needs a shot as well
and serves them quietly, as if unbidden,
as his nose-hairs twitch and crown bows low.
He serves, then sends them back into the world,
its winter snow-light and the crooked streets
where each of them must live forever and a day.

In the Library After Hours

That's Mrs. Willoughby, the blue-haired lady
who adores this shift.
She moves among a hundred thousand books
she never reads. Her job's
to whisk the many-colored spines.
When doors are locked, you hear her talking
loudly to the authors. Why, she wonders,
did they choose to spend their lives like this?
She knows that few of them
have been withdrawn in countless years,
and most will languish in the bookish dark
of decades, crumble into fly-dust,
molder into pulp. It's just
the physics of the thing, of course.
Some reply to her in whispers,
swear they don't mind isolation.
Few of them would take back what they gave
(or tried to give) to eyes and ears:
so many pages covered with their love
and fury, which the world ignored. It was quite
all right, it was, they tell her,
as her duster tickles their dry spines.
She nods. Sometimes she laughs at their
pretention and the waste of trees.

Some Effects of Global Warming
in Lackawanna County

The maples sweat now, out of season.
Buds pop eyes in wintry bushes
as the birds arrive, not having checked
the calendars or clocks. They scramble
in the frost for seeds, while underground
a sobbing starts in roots and tubers.
Ice cracks easily along the bank.
It slides in gullies where a bear, still groggy,
steps through coiled wire of the weeds.
Kids in T-shirts run to school, unaware
that summer is a long way off.
Their teachers flirt with off-the-wall assignments,
drum their fingers on the sweaty desktops.
As for me, my heart leaps high—
a deer escaping from the crosshairs,
skipping over barely frozen water
as the surface bends and splinters underfoot.

Below Zero

Ice petals on the trees.
The peppery black sparrows pour across
the frozen lawn.
The wind waits patiently behind the barn.

Though I'm not myself here, that's okay.
I've lost my name,
my last address, the problem
that has kept me up all night this week in winter.

Such a long time coming,
this white timeless time in time,
with zero to the bone
the best thing anyone could ever say.

I stand here in the open,
full of straw, loose-limbed, unmuffled.
No one's here, not-me as well,
this winter morning that goes on forever.

The Language of Mines

Impossible to write
without the culm dumps glowing at the edges
of the county line.
And difficult to think beyond the cellars
of our houses in West Scranton,
where the coal bins glistened with black ice.
The anthracite of meaning can't be dug
without a shovel. Words
are picks, sharp axes, spades.
We look to heaven as the last resort
but still those thunderheads grow bruises
over low-slung Lackawanna hills.
The winds crawl slowly with their sulfur fumes.
A burnt-out breaker just behind our school
adds little to this blue-bleak world
except the embers of what happened,
how the ground once gave us so much more.
We're full of grand abstractions now
in far-off cities of another plain.
We've all gone elsewhere just to dig.

The Grammar of Affection

Historiography 101

We can change the past but nothing more,
not this blind present or the things to come.

The moment breaks before us, blurs.
What's now is here.
It's history that anyone can fix:
the dead demand our strong revisions.

They'll only haunt us if we don't,
will hunt us down,
just as old selves will feed to frenzy
if we don't change everything they've said
or thought or done, add verses
to the chorus, modify refrains.

There's hope in history, my dear,
and one day anything can happen,
when it's ours again, to have and hold,
to cherish with the changes time will tell,
then tell again,
and each retelling with a clean, new music,
freshly scored, with skip and flutter of new life.

If anything could happen, then it surely did.
We can make it over as we make it up:
the past is all we ever have to live.

The Grammar of Affection

Without syntax there is no immortality,
       says my friend,
who has counted beads along a string
and understood that time is
            water in a brook
            or words in passage,
            caravans amid the whitest dunes,
            a team of horses in the mountain trace.

There is always movement, muttering,
       in flight to wisdom,
which cannot be fixed. The kingdom
       comes but gradually,
breaking word by wing or day by dream.

We proceed on insufficient knowledge,
trusting in what comes, in what comes down
       in winding corridors,
       in clamorous big rooms,
       above a gorge on windy cliffs.

In places where discovered sounds make sense,
where subjects run through verbs
to matter in the end, a natural completion
in the holy object of affections
as our sentence circles round again:

This grammar holds us, makes us shine.

To Ezra Pound

Venice, 1969

On the Calle dei Fabbri, in ripening dusk,
I heard you coming:
glib old geezer almost eighty-five.
You passed my table leaning on your stick,
repeating in a whisper broken lines:
Nel dritto mezzo…
while I sipped espresso,
writing in a notebook thick with silence,
filling up a void with my own chat.

Frail grizzly red-beard, Barbaroso
in a wide-brimmed hat and velvet cloak,
you swished beside me
reeking of old wax and brittle parchment.

And the bells above San Marco beat;
Venetian side-streets folded on themselves,
hexangular in shadows, smoke-light,
lapping water, low-hung skies,
with claims and counterclaims
that trailed behind you as before
through rambling decades as you fought
for this or that lost cause,
some odd, some noble, some unhinged.

Cui dono lepidum novum libellum?

You asked a number of good questions,

wading into dusk through scattered passages.
You were still afraid of what-comes-next,
that room of readers, large or small,
no consolation for the motley decades,
what was said and done, undone.

You saw the silver underside of heaven,
writing in your cage through nights in Pisa,
shivering in black rain of your making
as you cursed the economics of another age,
that bitch gone sour, tooth and gum,
with profits taken though of course unearned.

It was not enough to run the numbers
when so many died—mothers and fathers
with their daughters, sons, in blood-whelmed camps—
Nel dritto mezzo del campo e maligno
and the pits were *largo e profondo.*

Ezra, dwindling compound ghost:
you never understood that God is everywhere,
and all vengeance must belong to him.

Song and Skin

In the soft and quiet amplitude of dawn,
I wait beside a window.
Not sleeping well these days,
I wake in wonder
as the sun rims red the east-view hills;
cacophony begins with birds
and thoughts.
                    Pull down thy vanity,
I say aloud. So listening begins.

A voice starts low,
not mine so much as nothing in itself,
and which a holy man I met one day
called God, the not-self rising, rinsed by dawn,
almost laid bare.

Uncovered and alert,
I love whatever I can almost hear, a longing
satisfied in song and skin:
like something that I have in my possession
yet I still desire,
a wish to own what is mine already.

Unpatriotic Gore

It's true I never loved my country
in the abstract sense: red, white, or blue.
I have only this black waving flag,
my disposition.
Stars, bold stripes,
remind me of a million dead young men
in far-off ditches,
remind me of the innocents who fell,
collaterally damaged,
wild-eyed, blazing: each of them
a universe unmade.
I say that I have never loved my country,
but I'd surely die
for several good friends, my wife and sons.
I'd sacrifice a number of pink toes
and fingers, too (my own)
for Emerson, for Whitman and Thoreau.
I'd give an eye for one deep lake,
for several good streams,
at least one waterfall,
a lovely stand of Norway pines
just east of here, not far away.

The Lost Poems

I mourn those lost and lovely poems,
the ones not written,
left to founder in the faze of time.

They came too easily, perhaps:
the fragrant lines, the granite images,
all the lively phrases never turned to sums.

They felt as real as what I write now,
maybe more so,
being fragmentary, flushed, aflame.

They came and went
as I stepped awkwardly into a bath
or looked around me on the gravel path
or turned my back toward a wall of sleep.

Their vanishing was eerily complete.

It took so little just to lose their thread,
and I'm still missing what was almost said.

Toward a Poetics of the Next Generation

The poem of tomorrow won't be pretty.
It will clean the toilets with its flush,
a rude acidic caustic swirl.
It will dream in macroeconomic terms:
not single markets but a massive whole,
with aggregated indicators, models
of a complex world that churns in systems
larger than a single mind can dream.
It will think of capital and long-term growth,
enjoy the overview but like details,
the one-by-ones or two-by-twos,
like Noah's animals in arks of verse.
It will need the facts, but never fret.
The poem of the future will be radiant
with those particulars and wear its feelings
on its cuffs, a motley coat of many colors,
patchwork language gaudily displayed.
The poem of the future will adore
all humid luscious local gossip.
Yet its sadness will be global when
alas it takes to heart the end of green,
regards whole forests in decline,
the oily rivers where the bloated fish
rise to the surface with an eye
turned upward to a sun that beads it,
breaks it into many gleaming parts,
with noisy flies that feed to frenzy.
It will sing, of course, and celebrate, of course,
but not itself. No! Anything but that!
It will move beyond the tightness of the skin,

will open into air, its tingling gases.
It will dig beneath tectonic plates
to find that infamously molten core.
It will slither backward through the phyla
and approach beginnings, dawn-like pools
where ganglia begin to grow like cultures
in a petri dish, where consciousness itself
evolves from matter like a flame that breaks
from coal, a blue-vermillion tongue that lashes,
leaps—the sparks that breach a synapse.
It will make the universe its theme:
Why is there something in this space at all
and not just nothing, with its gap-toothed grin?
Is space just time hung to dry?
The poem of the future will attract detractors,
as it really must. It always must.
Some readers will be left, and far behind.
They'll prattle on about the garden,
and will find a spot of time to cherish
and specific places on a crinkled map.
But poems of the future must break free
of self and place. And even politics will seem
a petty adjunct to the world they rumble
with their harsh new syllables of dislocation,
voices in some register of sound
inaudible to everyone except the wolves,
who will come running from the farthest steppes
through evergreen and icy valleys
with their heat of breath and razor teeth.

Poem with Allusions

The thoughts that come on little cat feet
aren't mine, of course.
I'm prey to everything they've said,
and must believe in heaven and its hymns.
I've made my way through Chapman's Homer
and was so impressed.
I've watched my hands, like ragged claws,
crawl over you at night.
You didn't seem to mind.
You've read a lot and heard a lot.
We all have, dear.
We don't know who said what to whom
or why or when. The faces in the metro
look the same, each having been
through birth and copulation, even death itself.
I'd not thought death undid so many.
In country churchyards on the mossy stones,
their epitaphs may not impress the critics,
but they won't much care.

Lend an Ear

In winter, in the woods:
it's just me talking in my head.
I'm the noisy one among these pines.

And then a blackbird, with its charcoal eye,
burns through silence,
lifts a little song into the air.

Soft woods scrape.
I hear the shuffle of loose limbs,
the whiffing snow.

A breeze begins.
Begins and ends with nothing in-between
its bitter huffs.

I move along the ground,
through wiry brush, picking my way,
talking my way

through quiet stretches, word
by word, building a path
toward an opening, where I might say

some things that matter,
fill a silence that insists
in sounding like itself and nothing more.

But saying isn't said.
A listening air around me rises
as I lend an ear.

Hunch

I follow it, the snail of thought
I leave the track, turn off this trail
I crouch in shadows, under ferns
I refuse to answer every bird
I see the liquid glister in its shell
I taste the wind
I smell the smoke of fire in the woods
I hear the crackle of a thousand thorns
I feel the temperature rising
I consider every option valid
I attend each phase
I crumble into wet, black ground
I lose my place in sand and gravel
I listen for the clash of weeds
I wonder where the snail will go today

Revolutionary Days

All the little notions walk the streets
in scarlet dresses, dressed to kill,
while big and lumbering fresh thoughts
take off their shirts,
their muscles flexing in the midday sun.
The best of guesses strut their stuff,
in alleyways, in sad cafés,
while intimations slink, as ever,
in the cellar dark,
in chapels where the choir never sings;
their books are passed beneath the tables,
and there's someone singing out of tune
on some blue stage, in smoky light.
The worn-out theories of the old regime
are running scared now
over desert roads, on mountain passes,
hoping they will reach the border safely,
well before the posse
with their rifle-bright ideas
finds them in their flight and picks them off.

Bitch My Tongue

Tongue, bitch my tongue,
how I despise you
when you won't stand up, won't say
the worst, can't say it—
how the cities swarm,
whole continents of pain still fester,
little children broken into bits,
with old men strung in ribbons
on the barbs of fences by a stinking ditch.
I hate it when you won't say
souls are churning side by side
and hell seems air-conditioned
when compared to those hot rooms.
Can't say it, what goes on,
what sad unspeakable and sweaty
corridors are walked now
but without you, bitch my tongue
rising to clarify, denounce, deride.
Sometimes I want a decent butcher.
I would cut you out,
then wrap you in the filthy papers,
chuck you in the street
where dogs can have their fill of you.
Even mere silence wouldn't hurt as much,
would seem respectable
compared to what I'm forced to carry
in this big and silent mouth of mine.

At the Opening

I walked into the only open gallery
in this fair city.

Walls were white, so wide and empty.
Every frame was gilt.
The ceiling lofted, high and mighty.
Floors shone waxy hardwood clean.

I stood among a row of gawkers gawking
and could feel my legs grow wobbly and so long.
I rubbed my eyes to waken deeper.

There was so much here I couldn't see.
The artist (who wore white, with fiery wings)
seemed flighty, but I understood his pain.

It's never easy to see nothing clearly.

He could add so little to the world outside,
its myriad of streets, the great bazaar.
His emptiness was here, almost complete,
so beautifully hung, so bright, so dear.

Ars Poetica

Nonetheless the clouds go where they will
and as they will. There's no direction.

This does not, however, argue that the gods
are dead. Far from it. See them struggle

to contend with matter. We could matter less
and go our own ways promptly.

But the heavens want us badly in their fold.
They want the whole damn thing to matter.

Mostly we believe the clocks must tick, the skies
must open, seas must churn the same old stories,

lapping up shores like some good meal.
A few of us, however, sweep the world

with zigzag lightning of rude thoughts.
Low little gods, we make the page

a broad expanse where we rule roughly,
shifting things and words behind the things.

It's heavy work, but someone has to do it.
Somebody must rumble and contend.

Woman by the Way

I passed a woman on my way to work.
She didn't notice me, or so I thought.
She was in her garden clipping flowers.
Her hair was braided, dirty blond.
She wore a nightdress that was pink and white.
I guessed that she was nineteen, maybe twenty.
But my guess was wrong. I met her
later when a cinder hit my eye.
She was a doctor. You will be okay,
she said to me with such a weight of knowledge
I was quite relieved. I went home giddily
and late that night went out to water
all the little flowers along my path.

The Interruption of Summer

I should have known it, that a swooping jay
would interrupt this ease
with its bleak scold, blue-lightning screech,
and yet I didn't. I'm a fool, of course.
Been here all morning at eye-level
with the bloom of earth,
a sloping lawn,
this golden-green and summery resolve
of August where I sit,
with dandelion bursts and chicory and rue
attracting butterflies and bees
beneath the high black arms of locusts,
birches with their leaves like perfect hands
that wave a little in the slightest winds
to say they're real, that I'm real, too.

The jay came shooting from a height
like sudden pain,
a cold remembered January cry
that locked the world in iron lace
and kept me from my Adirondack chair,
this closeness to the grass, its soft serene,
the cool brown dirt my bare feet feel.
But everything is what it is, must be,
this passing paradise,
a sun-begotten honeyed August day:
unbidden, born again, beheld.
And maybe in the dream of some gold time
it will be mine to have again and hold,
with *always* as the part of speech
most prized yet purchased at a hefty price.

A Single Page

With a single page to write on,
what's to say?
Ten thousand things cannot be named.

Review the history:
you went out early in your life,
heard only snatches of the conversation,
and could not believe most things they said.

You went along with all the talk,
and nodded as you listened.
Nobody would ask you much about yourself,
and that was cool.

It was fairly quiet in the middle years,
and almost easy just to disappear,
to fold the tents of your big ears
and hang about the fringes in your slippers,
asking little of the world except
soft breezes, maybe susurration.

But a wild-ass wind shook all things loose,
your hair and shingles, shutters;
lids blew off the barrels in the yard
as winter showed you its hard face,
its sharp-toothed stare.

At times you wanted to despair,
yet what goes round comes round again.
Thermodynamics rescued you:
God knows that nothing's ever lost
that once was found.

You believe this now,
and many pages would add little
to what can be said within these margins:
borderless, unbound.

Ordinary Time

Magi

In the iron winter days
we sense them moving on bare hills
like inklings, omens:
wise ones coming from afar
with eager sun-dried faces
under heavy brows,
their curiosity a thing of wonder.

They've been riding hard for months
on lumpy camels,
with a growing certainty that's patience
magnified by faith in what will come,
now fixing on a star
that hovers in their brains
above a barn, far out of sight.

Our prayers have failed us,
so we listen as we wait for them,
this company of allies, aids
on this blue-bleak midwinter
where—in silence we have not imagined,
in its frost of solitude—
they will find us waiting:

For the desert wisdom of their coming.
For their slice of light on sand,
the purple shadows and the scent of grapes,
the blood-bright juice
that brings us faithfully again together
in this room of need, where
surely they find us—kneeling, still.

Heat Lightning

It's never heard, and keeps its distance,
never strikes a pig, a rosebush, or a barn.
A golfer on the green need not lie down
when it begins its horizontal crawl,
nor should the children scurry under trees
or swimmers panic as they head to shore.
Heat lightning happens over shoulders
in the middle distance, gleams the hills:
a shudder at the zinc-gray edge of daylight,
quietly assertive and yet indistinct,
a boom or tingle on the other side.
It's always elsewhere, rarely worth a sigh,
yet vaguely present on the ghostly rim
of weary minds. At night, it sometimes flickers
on the wall like lurid, passing headlights,
but you say that no one's really there,
no friend or enemy to call your name
outside the window, or to call you down.
It doesn't really care much if you care,
make sacrifices, pray, or change your ways.
It's glimmerings will find you unawares,
not ready to go home or go to sleep.
So just pretend it's not your business
and walk away. Walk quietly. Walk on.

Belief

Belief is fool's gold,
Aloysius said. I left the table,
as my pockets jingled,
and it's never good to argue
at a meal. I believe
a holy fool is rich,
and, there, I've said it.
So he welcomes evening sun,
believing that his star
will rise forever.
He sleeps so well
among the sodden logs
that lie beside the sea,
that suck and sink
all night in sand, too deep
to find him without digging.
And he blinks through morning
over quiet breakfast
on the glassy beach
that lifts him up.
Over simple lunch, he grazes
slowly as he reads his sutras,
or he gives and takes
among the troubled ones
he knows, and they are legion.
But he talks them through,
as he has hours to give away.
The afternoon may find him
sleeping as the tide slips in.
He's spindrift, foam-foot.
Oystercatchers call him

cheep, cheep, cheep.
His mind is golden wrack
and salt-weed, caught
and coiled among the jawbones,
exoskeletons of craw.
These shreds don't faze him,
as he's moving on,
and sleep's unreason rolls
him back to his belonging.

He believes that dreams
tell goodly tales. And so he listens,
learns in sleeping that the only story
is the one he's known
and told again, sung slowly
in the hollow conch,
the hocus pocus of the holy meal
taken together
on the long, white cloud
where each will gather
in a brave communion of pure souls,
conjoined and dancing
on the sand at sunrise
or around the fiery pit at night,
these goodly natives
of the world we win and lose,
win back each day
from morning into smoke-fall
dusk, from wine dark wane
to everlasting dawn.

Sisters of No Mercy

In a chalk-dust crypt in Sicily I saw them:
sisters of no mercy laid to rest
and buried with the merciful upon them,
old bones layered white on white.

How, after time, their body-wraps dissolve,
with insects picking clean old skin:
the stacked and musty skeletal remains
hide in abeyance in the vaulted dark.

The merciful had mercy in their hearts:
O blessed and beautiful their kindness
to themselves and to those sisters
who could not believe their own sweet hearts.

Midrash

Voltaire once said
that all the arguments for God's existence
hardly add a thing to what
we know already, being here.
We've walked in corn rows in midsummer,
seen the field aflame.
Even in winter there was
light enough to satisfy our need
for reassurance. God is
everywhere in wild abundance.
He waves from terraces or even cries
from windows in the alley.
Wants us to believe in yellow beams
that fall across the floor,
the doughy light of mild mid-day,
the slough of afternoon's blue shade
or fireflies popping in the dusky hedges.
He would have us breathe slow breath.
And somewhere in the rooms of this big house,
he's singing without words
in brilliant passages
that find us even without looking.
Soon his grace-notes gladden us,
the humming mind within our mind.

Aristotle in the Middle Ages

They came from everywhere to that long table
in the Middle Ages.
It was cold in damp Toledo
in the room where Bishop Raymond and the others
picked their way through tomes
now thick with dust-motes,
candles burning down the darkest time.
They could not believe their dizzy luck.
De Anima in Arabic was theirs,
his animation of the hard, true world
the soul inhabits like their feet in socks.
The nature of the natural was given
in a dozen works that God himself
could understand as what he really meant.
Having made their way down nights
through untold pages, with their quills alight,
they all went out into the little streets
to feed on sausages like fat red fingers
and to drink their health:
the world was theirs again to witness,
walk on, wake in, feed and feel.

The Poor at Heart

"So the last shall be first."

—MATTHEW 20:16

They scuttle under bridges, decks,
while bricks are falling through the floors,
and everything comes down around their ears.
They rest like crows on broken fences.
Uneven breaths disturb the air,
approximating wind. The grubby hands
reach up from rubble at the roadside.
Bodies at the margins stink in suns.
They smell of sour dust and shadow
and the shuck of palms.
Their still sad music moans around us,
pouring into ditches, over broken ground.

The bored reporters tell their stories,
but there's not enough of human
interest in so much dross
to sell more papers, as they must.
Some say that help is coming soon.
There may be medicine without borders,
ceremonies lifting them on high.
But priests and doctors in their shiny coats
are truly stumped. The macroeconomic
theories fail, with everyone
at last still waiting for the first,
with blue notes rising in the sooty air.

The Dissolution

It's snowing, and the world will soon be gone,
obliterated, blank
as what God started with before the itch
to just do something: *fiat lux.*

That blunt command
soon led to moorland, rock-ledge, seas,
to rivering blue canyons and the wildest steppes,
to guns and butter,
whispers of allegiance, longish kisses.

Now it's snowing hard.
And first the mountaintops dissolve.
Then tree-lines drop their hems and fade.
The barns go next.
Soon all the chickens come to roost

in your white house,
which will be gone as well with everything
around you: fingers, toes,
and finally your heart, its ticking
like a bomb that's muffled deep before it fades.

It must so be quiet everywhere again,
and without form
and maybe void as well, so rudely
empty of the things you love.
But everything comes back again, you know it.
In your bones you know it's true.
So *fiat nox.*

Ordinary Time

Days come and go:
this bird by minute, hour by leaf,
a calendar of loss.

I shift through woods, sifting
the air for August cadences
and walk beyond the boundaries I've kept

for months, past loose stone walls,
the fences breaking into sticks,
the poems always spilling into prose.

A low sweet meadow full of stars
beyond the margin
fills with big-boned, steaming mares.

The skies above are bruised like fruit,
their juices running,
black-veined marble of regret.

The road gusts sideways:
sassafras and rue.
A warbler warbles.

Did I wake the night through?
Walk through sleeping?
Shuffle for another way to mourn?

Dawn pinks up.
In sparking grass I find beginnings.
I was cradled here.

I gabbled and I spun.
And gradually the many men inside me
found their names,

acquired definition, points of view.
There was much to say,
not all of it untrue.

As the faithful seasons fell away,
I followed till my thoughts
inhabited a tree of thorns

that grew in muck of my own making.
Yet I was lifted and laid bare.
I hung there weakly: crossed, crossed-out.

At first I didn't know
a voice inside me speaking low.
I stumbled in my way.

But now these hours that can't be counted
find me fresh, this ordinary time
like kingdom come.

In clarity of dawn,
I fill my lungs, a summer-full of breaths.
The great field holds the wind, and sways.

Creed

I believe in him, my father, who came down from Scranton
with a brand new wife to Exeter, PA—
to have her and to hold till death did part.

I believe in all their sons and daughters
to the end of time and farther on.

I believe in every living thing, especially
the worms that make their way through seasons
of the skin, by light or shade, digging small runnels
in the soil and subsoil, knowing
that the birds won't find them easily
and change their slither-world again.

I believe in change as well, however painful.
It's where we live, my good friend says:
always eternal in the moment's burn
if not burned out by calendars, a waste of pages.

I believe in stars that dangle over
barns and burrows, ditches, scummy ponds;
I believe in keepers of the watch by night,
those lonely shepherds and their sheep who graze,
their wild-eyed children who rise up to live
and learn by several degrees of chance,
becoming what they must become by choice
or merely accidents of time and place.

Signore, I believe in almost everything
except in those who can't believe, who say
that he is dead, my only father, who came down
from Scranton on the drizzle-cloud of his unknowing
and gave life to me, which I pass on.

God's Operation on Adam

I'll take that rib while he's asleep.
He'll never miss it
and will soon prefer its newfound shape,
its whispers and concerns,
its wise and withering asides,
its interest in future generations.

Oh, I like the sound of this already.
If I had a rib, I'd give it up—
a fair exchange for so much bounty.
I would crown that crooked timber of a bone
with so much glory
you would almost think that she was God.

The Insomniac Thinks of God

Midwinter, after midnight:
coy-dogs shrill the bitter valley
as the owl, in moon-tones,
wonders who. Far off,
the lonely engine of a plane drones on.

It's then I think of him
who, unlike me, is without boundaries,
who, unlike me, can hold his tongue.
He listens urgently,
whose wakeful ear outlasts the night.

Dead Reckoning

In a red November's sunset mood
I move among the dead in this late wood,
old friends or family: a world gone by—
their dates, encapsulated, lifted high.
They shine around me, infinitely full
of what they were. One of them, a fool,
grins stupidly from distant ear to ear.
I'm silly as a boy when he comes near
with his loose tongue, those sassy lips,
a bag of tricks and well-worn quips.
One ghostly girl breaks down in silt,
her smell of mud, sharp taste of salt:
all shade and shadow, dangling vines
and roots that dig into the moldy, pine-
tar soil. It's painful to recall her fleshly ways,
the lilting manner of her easy sway,
her snow-bright bloom, or how she balanced
in the high-wire winds I rarely chanced.
I walk among the long familiar shades—
progenitors, accomplices, and aides.
Like there, my father, in a sandy mound,
his love like water running underground.
He takes a quiet place among these dead,
these whisperers in my unquiet head,
who sift in currents, humming in the wind,
and almost without bidding come to mind,
small lights that shimmer, lead me down
this dusky path so thickly overgrown
I have to wonder if I'll make it back
before the sun turns cindery and black.

Lament of the Middle Man

In late October in the park
the autumn's faults begin to show:
the houses suddenly go stark
beyond a thinning poplar row;
the edges of the leaves go brown
on every chestnut tree in town.

The croaking birds go south again
where I have gone in better times;
the hardy ones, perhaps, remain
to nestle in the snowy pines.
I think of one bold, raucous bird
whose wintry song I've often heard.

I live among so many things
that flash and fade, that come and go.
One never knows what season brings relief
and which will merely show
how difficult it is to span
a life, given the Fall of Man.

The old ones dawdle on a bench,
and young ones drool into their bibs;
an idle boffer, quite a mensch,
moves fast among the crowd with fibs.
A painted lady hangs upon
his word as if his sword was drawn.

Among so many falling fast
I sometimes wonder why I care;
the first, as ever, shall be last;

the last are always hard to bear.
I never know if I should stay
to see what ails the livelong day.

I never quite know how to ask
why some men wear bright, silver wings
while others, equal to the task,
must play the role of underlings.
"It's what you know, not who," they swore.
I should have known what to ignore.

I started early, did my bit
for freedom and the right to pray.
I leaned a little on my wit,
and learned the sort of thing to say,
yet here I am, unsatisfied
and certain all my elders lied.

A middle man in middle way
between the darkness and the dark,
the seasons have tremendous sway:
I change like chestnuts in the park.
Come winter, I'll be branches, bones;
come spring, a wetness over stones.

Spring Burials

In the north-world, wild with patience,
spring arrives with opening of graves.
The bodies have been warehoused
throughout winter,
stacked and stiff: sad remnants
that could hold a life together
in the better days.
Brought out of store,
they settle in their fresh-cut cubicles of loam,
which after all must feel like home
to those who lay them there at last.

Eternal Tailor

Was that my tie? It might have been
my father's, with those bold magenta dots,
too loud for me, so frayed and soiled.

The loose threads separate, stick out:
I hate to pull them, but I must.
This sweater-vest is old in any case.

A shoelace opens. Will I let it drag?
My bottom sole's becoming free,
a loose-flapped, almost silly tongue.

This shirt has way too many tears;
the ring around the neck is not my own.
And yes I don't care what they say.

All circles start somewhere, of course.
They grow around my eyes and belly.
There is more and less of me today

than I'm prepared to measure with a tape.
My fingernails and bones are brittle, breaking,
not the strongest fabrics in the world.

Eternal Tailor of this suit of age,
go dress another one, for we are many,
though I can't take comfort from this crowd.

Do Lord Remember

Do Lord remember. I remember you.
The petals of the pear tree you devised,
soft blasts of light, blown white-asunder,
heaps of blossoms on the grass around.
The long hot summers sing your praises:
all the lapping seaside shorelines,
black rocks breaking through the surf like you
break out so boldly in the slosh of waves.
The oystercatchers always own your call.
Each butterfly is yours, each moth and mouse.
Each firefly, too, now popping in the dusk
or, half-remembered, popping in my head.
The fall is yours, that tumbling season,
with its mold and mulch, its yellow paths
through mind-ways opened and pursued.
You made the crystals on the parlor pane,
those dazzle-diagrams and fractal flares.
I do remember you in every month.
I'm not forgetful, like my foolish friend
who lost his memory midway and fell.
I'm not that old and toothless woman
I have watched go down your garden path.
It's quite a massacre, I must confess:
the dying generations, child by man,
the women disassembled one by one,
dear wives and daughters, mothers of us all.
I'm guessing you require so much destruction
just because you can, as doing does.
Don't get me wrong—my tone tips over
once or twice a day to snarky digging—

but I do intend no disrespect.
I believe in you, the ways you went,
your hands that lifted me along the hills,
that pointed out (in case I didn't notice)
many sudden turns I should have seen
but almost didn't. You have never failed me,
though I know I sometimes pissed you off.
I believe I'm coming back to you again
one day beside myself, perhaps in glory
or, if less dramatic, as a snail or slug,
a butterfly or bee, an aardvark or a dog.

You have kindly shown me how it's done,
and daily resurrections get me going.
I have learned to ride slow waves to shore.
There may be other tricks I've learned as well
in this good time we've been together.
Life is harder than at first I knew;
the course is long, blood-soaked, or worse.
I sometimes hesitate or stop to sigh.
Do Lord remember that I'm only human.
I have faults you've never seen before.
There's probably a touch of hubris there,
but let it ride. You're good at that, I hear.
Do Lord remember me as I do you.

Old Frogs

for Norman MacCaig

I take some comfort from old frogs
who squat around the pond
like bodhisattvas, contemplating
nothing but their own exclusion
from the world beyond them, falling
deeper into selfless
silence and the dereliction
of all duty but to sit like this,
apart from offspring
leaping in the air or falling
through their parachutes of flesh
or dying on the road like Jesus,
with their arms outstretched.
Articulate composure
is their mode, as unheroic as
the rocks around them,
clumped and cooling as the night comes on.

Blessings

Blessings for these things:
the dandelion greens I picked in summer
and would douse with vinegar and oil
at grandma's little house in Pennsylvania,
near the river. Or the small potatoes
she would spade to boil and butter,
which I ate like fruit with greasy fingers.

Blessings for my friend, thirteen
that summer when we prayed by diving from a cliff
on Sunday mornings in the church
of mud and pebbles, foam and moss.
I will not forget the fizz and tingle,
sunning in wet skin on flat, cool rocks,
so drenched in summer.

And for you, my love, blessings
for the times we lay so naked in a bed
without the sense of turbulence or tides.
I could just believe the softness of our skin,
those sheets like clouds,
how when the sunlight turned to roses,
neither of us dared to move or breathe.

Blessings on these things and more:
the rivers and the houses full of light,
the bitter weeds that taste like sun,
dirt-sweetened spuds,
the hard bright pebbles, spongy mosses,
lifting of our bodies into whiffs of cloud,
all sleep-warm pillows in the break of dawn.

from

The Art of Subtraction

(1998–2005)

After the Terror

Everything has changed, though nothing has.
They've changed the locks on almost every door,
and windows have been bolted just in case.

It's business as usual, someone says.
Is anybody left to mind the store?
Everything has changed, though nothing has.

The same old buildings huddle in the haze,
with faces at the windows, floor by floor,
the windows they have bolted just in case.

No cause for panic, they maintain, because
the streets go places they have been before.
Everything has changed, though nothing has.

We're still a country that is ruled by laws.
The system's working, and it's quite a bore
that windows have been bolted just in case.

Believe in victory and all that jazz.
Believe we're better off, that less is more.
Everything has changed, though nothing has.
The windows have been bolted just in case.

The Prophets

They come to us from elsewhere,
false and true,
some standing in the park on boxes, shouting,
some on buses, rising
to declare whatever moves them
to their calls for justice, retribution, mercy,
common sense. They bear
a message from the fourth dimension
of their clearest vision,
speaking to an age indifferent to reason.
It is hard to understand their grief,
their anger, and their joy.
A few disciples carry on behind them,
handing out the leaflets,
playing tapes, believing in belief.
Sad, how few words
are true enough to matter,
make us willing to attend a meeting,
answer calls, or rise above the crowd.

The Lost Soldiers

The dead and missing from the foreign wars
come home again.
They've been at sea these many years
in bunks, on deck
with cobalt waters underneath them sloshing;
scavengers, the gulls in their long wake
gobbling the body parts,
the bits and pieces cast adrift.
They roam our town in shredded uniforms
and dented helmets,
stand and stare in parks and public forums,
bleeding from the ears,
the stomach, at the neck,
but now and then
alert enough to raise a wary eyebrow,
wondering what cause
was just enough and equal to the terror
of the little children
who were burned, though probably in error.

Occupied Country

The bees now, zumming over flowers,
hesitate a moment, then pass on.
The children only dance indoors.

The government believes the worst about us.
They have put up signs:
Your neighbors may have come from somewhere else.

I'm looking over shoulders not my own.
I don't give out my number anymore.
I listen for the feet outside my door.

Sleeping Through the Storm

All night the black rain soaked my body.
I could not get up.
The lightning zigzagged through my brain.
I listened at the wall, where voices
indistinctly begged for their brief lives.
I tried to shout, but words like arrows
fell into the grass short of their target.
I could smell the bacon fat downstairs,
the dirty laundry in the wicker basket.
I could hear the little ones, upset.
The village idiot was at the door.
The fire department wanted me to dress
and join the company around the fire.
The armies of the night, like frenzied beetles,
marched on cities. Ants assembled
in a long red line, prepared to follow.
I could not get up.

Listening to the BBC World Service
Late at Night

My little radio, my shortwave
monster of confession,
small black box of many sorrows
and a joke or two:
it turns you on to brag about
destruction, tell me that
in jungles heads are rolling,
that the city towers tumble on themselves.
In deserts, things are even worse.
The children, too,
it seems, must suffer
as the world goes boom.
Sometimes I hate what you
have said, can't stop
from saying. I could fling you out
the window testily
in high green grass,
but everybody knows
you'd just keep squawking.
Better let you scream.

The President Eats Breakfast Alone

The president sips coffee, all alone
in his white house.
The cameras cannot invade his mind.

He doesn't understand why some won't cheer
when he cries war
against the enemies of right and good.

The bombs must fall. The helicopters must
arrive in clusters and conclude their efforts.
We will show real mercy in the end.

We don't want war, not war exactly,
he explains politely
to the other president who lives inside him.

He adjusts his tie.
We want the terror just to go away.
We are the terror, somebody has said.

How can that be? We're free and easy.
We have walked our little kids to school.
On Sundays, in the park, we toss the balls.

The president admires the silver spoon
beside his cup.
His room is cool and bright and quiet.

He has been elected, after all.
His body is a powerful machine.
His eyes are steady and his hands are clean.

Democracy

Near dusk, the vote is called.
So one hand rises, then another
in the pine-planked room of men and women,
as the little children suck their thumbs.

There is broad assent
among the many seated in the pews,
in balconies, on window ledges, standing at the back.

In shadow, there are those who disagree,
who hunch in anger, clutch their elbows,
tip their heads away from what was said.

A few of them will never leave this hall
until the darkness, which has just begun,
grows inside out,
and one by one they move into the night
with empty pockets, with a granite heart.

Fish-Eye View

Not everyone's so lucky.
Long before the world drew up its shades,
we gathered at the table, trembling,
and drew lots. A friend of mine,
who washed his hands before and after
every single meal, became an earthworm.
One, a teller of white lies,
now swings his guts
in some damp forest, limb to limb,
spinning his web. He's looking for
a fly who was my neighbor
in the mist before: always annoying
with his busy drone in my good ear.
That guy who hit on anything in skirts
is baying at the moon, far from the pack,
lost in the howl of his desire.
One girl who favored woolen sweaters
has become a moth in her own closet.
But I'm sitting pretty in Des Moines,
in this bright mall, one of a tank
of ritzy goldfish. Not so bad,
with easy money all around me,
and a gilded life for me to spend.

Peaches

With a ladder strung for me to climb,
the long branch quivering,
I rise toward them:
bright pink cheeks,
the globes that fill my eager palms
with their round wholeness,
palpable, improbably complete in morning
blaze of easy sun.
Their fragrance calms me.
Near them, all the world seems young,
so lovely,
light skin fuzzy on my tongue.

High School

Everyone must go there.
None returns.

One sees the boys get into line,
their first mustache more like a wish
above their lips. The girls stand
parallel and pure, some of them bleeding,
all of them afraid. They've seen

their older sisters taken. They have seen
their older brothers, too,
assimilated, saturated, swept.

The hot brick building is a kind of furnace.
They're its fuel.

The hot brick building is a kind of maw
that feeds to frenzy.

Everyone must go there.
None returns.

Family Reunion

So they arrive, the relatives again
in their tight shoes, the men with ties
as narrow as your finger,
shirts with shadows underneath the arms.
The women fill the doorframes with their hips.

They smell of fish, hot oil, and coffee.
One of them has wrung a chicken's neck
the night before and enters proudly
with her sloppy bag of broken wings
and breasts like hands folded in prayer.

The older women huddle in the den,
as round as ottomans,
these stumps of motherhood
without a pride of children at their feet.
They know the truth

about your uncle, who has not come in.
They know he lived as well as anyone
in that position could have lived,
given his lameness, deafness of an ear,
that turn of mind.

They just keep coming, even second cousins
twice removed. They're in your house
all day and night, spaghetti junction
of the roads you've travelled, more or less.
Their visit lasts, of course, forever.

Covenant in April

And so I make it with the ground itself,
which only deepens as I stand and dig,
this soil my home now, layer unto layer,
top and subsoil, crust and crumble.
Make it with the whole imagined earth
I catalogue by root and branch, by hand
and mouth, by what is said but mostly not.
With hard black coal that's hidden underneath,
immortal diamond-eye of truth.
With you, my star, that rises in the east
and takes a gaudy turn across the vault,
then settles into soft, alluvial terrain
in this wet month of pent-up buds,
when frivolous and fiery thoughts begin
and birds assemble, summoned from the south
like words almost forgotten but not quite.

Old Teams

Not one of them still walks among us,
who can stand and talk and bicker
and make love; they've lost their footing
in the world, gone under
pitch and pool, run off the tracks
where they once circled, golden-thighed
and sprightlier than crowds of lookers-on.
They're gone, the golfers in their wool plus-fours,
the divers in the suits with shoulder straps,
the quarterbacks in close-fit, leather helmets.

Looking in their eyes, behind the glass,
the glaze of decades, I can only wonder
what they make of me, this hovering
compassionate blank gaze from time beyond.
They would have to know
that I was coming, and that I would love them,
as I really do, for their blear innocence
and their fool faith in games to come.

Rise

One thing happens, then another.
In the long slow rise, so many hands
reach out and lift us
over fallen branches, hidden drops,
hard crops of stone. The moon
tilts up its yellow chin. The clouds
disperse. We grow into a face
our mothers recognize as someone else,
a father's father, sister's sister.
Nobody is single in this world.
That's all we know, will ever know,
about the ways we come and go.
We're pulled to presence by a doctor's
urgent, gentle hands; we're laid
to sleep and covered over. Nobody's
alone. I'm here with you. Here
reaching for your fingers, holding on.

The Broken Neck

Her frosty-headed husband roughly snoring
never moved but grumbled in his sleep
as she went down to feed the cat at midnight,
pausing at the dizzy top of stairs,
then pitching forward, falling through the dark
into the cellar, headfirst, landing on her face.
A cold, clay floor whirling around her,
she lay dead awake, and could sense
the lost years waiting with a cap in hand,
her head above the clouds, a blur below.
Her limbs were children in a heavy sleep,
remote beside her as she lay there thinking
all too clearly, with the cat's white tail
and purring engine settled at her neck.

Leo

You were here before me, Leo:
father and my son.

I see your circle as it shines
through sunny haze—

a large unbroken circle
that encloses all my days.

I come and go, dear Leo,
in a world below

your arcing rainbow.
I am lost and won.

I walk this passage in-between.
I'm seen, unseen.

But you are luminous,
enormous, porous

and surrounding name.
Your single flame

warms both my hands,
my either side

on this cold passage
through an age

where everyone was born
before they died.

Not you, my Leo:
here before me and long after,

fiery constellation,
father and my son.

The Trees Are Gone

Rebecca Avenue has lost its trees:
the willow that would brush against my window,
and the spruce that cooled our porch out back,
the ginkgo I would rake in mid-October,
with its matted leaves like Oriental fans.
Even the beech has been cut down,
that iron pillar of my mother's garden,
with its trunk so smooth against one's cheek.

The dirt I dug in has been spread
with blacktop: tar and oil. They've rolled it
blithely over sidewalk slate
where cracks once splintered into island tufts.
Even leafy hills beyond the town
have been developed, as they like to say:
those tinsel woods where I would rinse myself
in drizzle, in the pin-wheel fall.

You can stand all day here without knowing
that it once knew trees: green over green
but gamely turning violet at dusk,
then black to blue-vermillion in the dawn.
It's sentimental, but I miss those trees.
I'd like to slip back through the decades
into deep, lush days and lose myself again
in leaves like hands, wet thrash of leaves.

Borges in Scotland

In the dismal garden at Pilmour
I watched old Borges, blind man leaning
on his stick among the iron trunks of beech,
a wind-dark canopy of claws above him.

Gusts of salt wind swayed the trees,
rippling the feathers of the bracken floor.
"It's rooks," he said, ears opening like palms.
The empty headlights of his eyes turned up.

So Borges listened and was birds.
A soot-cloud rose, world-blackening,
the hard-by thunder of a thousand birds
who called his name now: Borges, Borges.

Mind

The wind knows nothing,
tossing every leaf and light blue hat
that it surrounds,
invisible but violent of purpose,
single-minded in its sweep
and unselective grasp of everything before.

The mind is like this,
moving forward, sideways, backwards
through the object-world,
undoing what was given, smothering,
unmaking in its wake, then making light
of its destruction, moving on.

Power Stations

You'd think that, from a height, they'd disappear,
but astronauts report you still can see them
when so many other vivid features
disappear from view: these ganglia of wire,
rods and pistons, conical high towers
rising in a forest or on distant plains,
elaborately hidden from the common view.

A few of them, like Three Mile Island or Chernobyl,
call attention to themselves like teens
who suddenly must walk on some wild side.
They ruin everything around them, fail
at school, wind up in rehab or the local jail.
Their reputations never will recover,
but their peers still hide and power on.

I came upon one in its monstrous glory
in the summer woods, leafing my way
through vast anthologies of heavy foliage.
For a brief while, standing in that vision,
I was all ablaze, part of its story.
Even now, far from that luminary site,
I feel the surge, the tingle, coming through.

Near Old Meldrum, After a Funeral

In memoriam Nick Bogdan

What a world, the godhead gone
but everywhere his bony little feet protruding,
blunt toes poking out from underneath
the blankets of the dawn,
the fields of rye.
His knobby knees stick out through ledges,
and his tongue's a lacerating stream
through woods in early spring.
Those are his shoulders lifting hedges,
hips that bulge the downy heath.
His fingers climb the walls of sky.

The Crucifixion

Woodmites burrowed through the beams,
delighting in the rot, the punky core.
A million ants marched up the hill,
lured by a honey-covered bun
dropped by a solider, who could only dream
about the distant province where his mother
drew sweet water from the well
and where his father followed in the tracks
his father cut through sugar-loam of fields.
Pickpockets moved among the crowds
that dwindled to a few by afternoon;
they'd had more luck the day before,
when somebody whose crimes were better known
was hung to dry. Against the sky,
a dozen vultures wondered if the wind
would bear them up
through this long day and those that followed,
if the feast below was worth the wait.

Late Thoughts

Impossible, the decades gone
with all the stars I've wished upon
still there. My wishing time is done.

From time to less of it, I leap
and learn a little what to keep
beside me. Down is always steep.

I fall. We all fall down at last,
turn every present into past
and wonder how it went so fast.

There's no one left but me and you,
it seems: a house, an empty shoe,
and nobody to say what's true

or false. Take what you need. No more.
Though no one's really keeping score.
Remember to pull shut the door.

The Art of Subtraction

In the afternoon, in summer,
sitting by the pond, I did the math.
Subtraction was
the next best thing to insight I could manage.

Take away the house, the tree, the bird.
Get rid of walls, real or imagined.
Look for less in everything around you.

I became a snail with nothing but my shell
to carry forward. It was not
as bad as maybe you might think.

I pared the dictionary down as well,
saved only nouns like stones along a path,
saved verbs that moved in one direction.
Ancillary parts of speech
seemed pointless and could go to hell.

I'm back this afternoon, in autumn,
sitting where I used to,
trying once again to clear my head,
subtract the last things I don't need,
get down to only
what cannot be shaken loose or said.

from

House of Days

(1989–1998)

Stars Falling

Fire-flakes, flints: the same old stars
still fiery in the unredemptive sky,
the silvery and hopeless midnight sky
that feels like home from here to Mars,
then gradually grows foreign into stars
we hardly recognize, that fill the eye
with lofty gleanings we ineptly scry
by framing legends of unending wars.

There is some comfort in the way they sprawl,
their vast composure in the cold and careless
spaces that absorb them as they fall,
their dwindling into dark with less and less
of anything a witness might recall,
the ease of their becoming homelessness.

Swimming After Thoughts

In memory of Robert Penn Warren

Across the blackened pond and back again,
he's swimming in an ether all his own;

lap after lap, he finds a groove
no champion of motion would approve,

since time and distance hardly cross his mind
except as something someone else might find

of interest. He swims and turns, eking
his way through frogspawn, lily pads, and shaking

reeds, a slow and lofty lolling stroke
that cunningly preserves what's left to stoke

his engines further, like a steamwheel plunging
through its loop of light. He knows that lunging

only breaks the arc of his full reach.
He pulls the long, slow oar of speech,

addressing camber-backed and copper fish;
the minnows darken like near wishes,

flash and fade—ideas in a haze of hopes
ungathered into syntax, sounding tropes.

The waterbugs pluck circles round his ears
while, overhead, a black hawk veers

to reappraise his slithering neck, and frogs
take sides on what or who he is: a log

or lanky, milk-white beast. He goes on swimming,
trolling in the green-dark glistening

silence and subtending mud where things
begin, where thoughts amass in broken rings

and surface, break to light, the brokered sound
of lost beginnings: fished for, found.

Rain Before Nightfall

Late August, and the long soft hills
are wet with light:
a silken dusk, with shifting thunder
in the middle distance. Chills
of fall have not yet quite
brought everything to ruin.
And I stop to look, to listen
under eaves. The yellow rain
slides down the lawn,
it feathers through the pine,
makes lilacs glisten,
all the waxy leaves. The air
is almost fit for drinking,
and my heart is drenched,
my thirst for something
more than I can see
is briefly quenched.

The Lake House in Autumn

There's silence in the house at summer's wake.
The last leaves fall in one night's wind,
the mice are eaten, and the cats begin
a rumbling sleep. There's nothing much at stake.
It's not quite cold enough to stoke
the furnace, and the neighbors never seem to mind
if leaves are raked. I'm staring through a blind
at less and less beside a cooling lake.

I keep forgetting that this absence, too,
must be imagined. What is still unknown
is still beyond me, as with you.
The mind is darker, deeper than a windblown
lake that tries to mirror every hue
of feeling as the season takes me down.

Willow Song

Willow, willow, drooping gold,
there is a story you have told
of how you cast your locks upon
a cold stream always passing on.
Your melancholic, bold display
of gravity throughout the day
is just the gesture to appall
the trees beside you standing tall
and primly saying nothing much.
They hate the way you seem to gush,
as if relief were to be found
in falling forward to the ground.
It makes them wince to see you bend;
they're wondering what you intend.
Your grief in gaudy limbs unfurled
like garments rent before the world
is just too much for them to take.
(They think, in fact, it's all a fake.)
But willow, willow, I'm with you.
If only I could cast my rue
in similarly lush cascades
of desperate, abandoned braids.

The Discipline of Seeing

How can you begin to say what's here?
In north New Hampshire woods turn rough
with jack pine, scrub oak, thistle;
granite edges flake in sunlight,
and the dirt is sandy, roots
like old hands swelling at the knuckles.
Air is white, and lakes are bluer:
pieces of old sky that fell to earth.
The wind seems far too high today
as white pines rustle at enormous height,
a lofty, lush, deep-throated whir;
its broad effects are all on view,
if only you can train the eye to watch,
to focus properly on what presents
itself in time, in taste and color,
shapes that shift from hill to valley
and demand continuous transcription.
It is always difficult to hold,
to place a moving landscape in the mind,
where language feeds upon the given world.

A Killing Frost

Beside the pond in late November,
I'm alone again
as apples drop in chilly woods
and crows pull tendons like new rubber
from a road-kill mass.

Ice begins to knit along the ground,
a bandage on the summer's wounds.
I touch the plait
of straw and leaf-mold, lingering to smell
the sweet cold crust.

An early moon is lost
in sheer reflection,
wandering, aloof and thinly clad,
its eye a squint of expectation.

And I know that way,
this looking for a place to land
where nothing gives,
these boundaries of frost and bone.

Who Owns the Land?

Who owns the land?

Not I, the sparrow.
I have seen it passing, and have dropped
to taste its lively worms. I've built a nest
in its red oak and fluttered in the sky
among my children as they learned to fly
above the field. We all have fed here.
Many of us died: so many feathers,
dust of wings.

Who owns the land?

Not I, the fox.
I merely hunt among its shadows.
In the land of snow, I leave my tracks.
In summer corn I pick my way.
I dig my holes, but I owe nothing
to the bank of fools. I borrow time.
I burrow and I bend to every season.
I will come and go, like you—and you.

Who owns the land?

Not I, the frog.
Even though I take my coloration
from the land I wear, that wears me out.
I merely swallow what the air provides:

a thousand wings, good taste of fly.
I'm hardly more than mud myself,
and nobody owns me.

Who owns the land?

Not I, not I.
I simply live here. Here I die.

Nature Revisited

A sparrow hawk has swooped,
a field mouse fails behind the Kmart
in the empty lot where dandelions sprout
in blacktop cracks.

The sun's gold kite is flying overhead,
monotonously high;
heat hangs like someone's bright idea
gone awry.

Hello, it's summer.
And the world is full of fiber optics.
Everyone's on-line, their email begging
for a rapid answer.

Mothers with their pudgy, fevered children
wait in corridors, in plastic chairs.
The intercom is talkative today.
The mothers pray

as fish are drying in the local streams,
and billboards shimmer.
Tar boils pop in fresh-laid roads
as cars slur by.

There's new construction going on quite near:
white glass and cinder block and steel.
The trucks like yellowjackets buzz;
they sting and disappear.

. . .

The sky is falling, piece by piece,
like weakened plaster.
It is hard to find the wilder world,
what nature was.

Look in the thickets of a thousand sorrows,
under bridges or behind the malls,
in hedgerows leading nowhere in the dust,
or over walls

for what is missing. It is there.
You'll see.
Hello, it's summer.
It is there. You'll see.

House of Days

1. JANUARY

The red fox picks its way.
It roots in gullies
for a nesting vole, a field mouse
stranded by the freeze.

All night the attic teemed with mice
like unformed thoughts,
their small feet crumbling through a thousand pages
of the boxed-up books I've never read.

The children are asleep,
their shallow breaths the rise and fall
of generations, though I know that winter
will consume them, fix their thoughts
(like mine this morning) on the only end,
when what is passing has been passed,
unhoused at last.

I look up from my desk:
the glassy light is hard to see through,
slantwise, chill.
The old white house grows whiter still.

There's silence in the sheets
that gather on my desk,
and I want to read somewhere of something

that is not this empty winter wait
for what will happen
in the wake of colder things to come.

2. FEBRUARY

A lace is spread
against the high black table of the night.

I'm walking in an orchard near my house
as stars detach and flutter into air.

The apple trees are bare,
but flakes are heaped like sugar on their limbs.

The roads are drifting deep with stars,
the ditches filling,

and the house dissolves—
the clapboards fading white on white.

In a blink, it's gone:
the life I knew,

till sweeping winds invent a syntax
I may try to use

to re-create my house,
its soft, bright lines,

floor after floor, the stanzas
rising through a snowy gauze,

the chimney poking through a scrim
of powder into hard, black time.

3. MARCH

The sun is cold and yellow
on my study wall.
I nose among the books,
those written and unwritten,
dust of thought that clings or passes.

Love that's come and gone
means less now,
though I wish I'd known when I was younger
that a simple phrase can last forever,
if it's only true.

Beyond my window, in the snowy field,
the sun has found reflected glory
I could never match.
I let that light fall on my page.

The way of silence is a lasting way,
a darker way,
but not this month this mood this matter
that I waste my heart on,
web of words, this still-becoming
text that's spun to catch whatever falls.

4. APRIL

The ice-floes shelve in alabaster streams,
and ground goes sodden underfoot.

Even the children start to turn,
their small tight fists becoming shovels
that can dig and dig.

My wife has changed her name again,
the letters on her skin,
as black-limbed hills begin to feed,
their long roots sucking.

There is just no end to what goes on.

5. MAY

Familiar tropings of a Spring Abstract:
the apple trees in bloom,
the house in gold, glad-handing light,
the garden path now fraught with bees.

Enough of that.
I put my face into the grass and breathe.
I root among the stones
and feel the singe of my own brightness,
light from light,
a speechless passage through a shimmer-time.

My project for the sun is more than words.
It involves this house,
now blazing whitely on the hill of noon.
It involves the bumblebee
that works its way from bloom to bloom.
It involves an urge to lift myself
beyond this frame,
beyond the difference of word and thing,

this pale Abstract,
the hackneyed rhythms we were born to sing
in Mary's month, *dum-derry-derry-ding*.

6. JUNE

The house is in a flush of expectation.

For the uncut grass,
which deepens into noon.

For tiny swallows bunched in eaves
or dipping through the dusk.

For the pond that rises, fed invisibly
from streams below, its fringe of weeds
lashed to and fro.

And for the children:
long legs running on the minty world,
immaculate before their fall to mud,
their graceless tumble
on the trek to home.

7. JULY

Here is the spark of heaven,
rising on the Fourth, the spangled night
of firefall flakes, the glitzy stars.

I let the pond uphold my spirits,
drunk with day's long exaltations,
floating on the raft of fellow-feeling

as the children swarm in rings around me
and the rockets spray.

The universe expands to fill my chest,
an outward crackle, ribs uncaged,
my bird-heart flown to God-knows-where.

The birth of freedom is my theme tonight,
the crack of rifles,
no more king, no taxes from abroad,
and each hand counts.

We'll tax ourselves from here on out.
We'll make ourselves the only kings.
We'll feed the people on the bread of truth.
We'll raise the children to believe for sure
that every color is divinely lit,
that every stone is God's own flint,
that free means free
not only here but there as well,
wherever in the world the star-flakes fall,
the moon is swelling,
and the ponds fill up and go on filling.

8. AUGUST

Bounty, bounty.

And the children multiply and feed
like loaves and fishes.
and the crickets thrum in weedy corners
but are not a plague.
The corn is high above our heads

and spilling into ears, so ripe and sweet.
The garden tumbles with its plenty:
beans, potatoes, peppers, kale.

Improbably
we sit and talk of cities
where the streets are hard,
the sidewalks slept on by a thousand souls
in coinless, dreamless, lamplit wonder.
We condemn the nights where crack is king,
where guts are shredded for the smallest change,
where Programs fail,
where death has lost the power of troping.

Nothing in the world outside this text,
I want to say.
I want this text to hold, to cover
bodies on the street.
I want it for a net to catch what falls.
I want it, like a spider's web, to shake
when any strand, oh anywhere, is touched.

9. SEPTEMBER

I saw it through a net of rain at dusk:
the field in fall,
its tearlike traceries against the pane.

The stones were sponges
left outside all night to drink,
the grass was sopping.
Leaves cut loose and flattened on the mud.

I could almost not believe the world
beyond those fields:
the God-abandoned gullies, cliffs of fear,
the deadhead swamps,
streams disappearing into deeper woods.

I put a log on,
watched it waken into flame.
I felt the warmth, the hiss to crackle,
fall to fire,
while somewhere overhead
the black geese flew, V after V,
a honking wedge of autumn knowledge
I would never have.

Their south was simile to me, no more;
their teleology was not my own.
I was here, and winterbound, and staying—
though the leaves went brown and visions failed
in traceries, in tears.

10. OCTOBER

Leafmeal, gild: the glory of a wood
too deep in dying to rehearse old times.
The tinsel days are full of flutter,
an advancing wind like military drums
before the slaughter of a billion lives.
We've come to die, but nobody complains
as bannerols are flown, as flags go snap.
The General is waving from his hill,
is mounted on his high, white horse of clouds.
There's rock and drill, a draft of courage,

bugles like we've never heard before.
The death of dying is the only death
that matters, but it's not within
our purview now; this loud, full battle
has our eyes, our ears in thrall;
we're ankle-deep in all these corpses,
mulch and mangle, in the fell of fall.

11. NOVEMBER

The cellarhole is filled with dark,
the smell of apples rotting in a bin,
the stench of clay.
I sweep my hand through cobwebs streaming
from the joists and rafters
to adjust the settings on the furnace.
Old pipes hiss.

I climb the stairwell into light again,
a kitchen lit by lemons in a bowl,
by late November's pooling light.

The children will be waking soon,
but I have time to squeeze the oranges
and pour the milk, remembering
the way my father rose without a clock,
and always dark. He'd stoke
the fire with chunks of coal,
then lay our boots out, pair by pair,
and stir the porridge over glass-blue flame.

These daily turns are what sustain me
through the passing days

as I ascend the spiral of each season,
reaching upward to the rosy light,
the only sun that can sustain me
in the world above,
beyond this rude vernacular that plays
for time, this temporizing phase,
beyond the circle of repeating days.

12. DECEMBER

The children have all left.
Their beds are empty, and the drawers hang out.
The bowls and spoons no longer chatter.

I have read the books along that shelf
beside the window.

Each of them is full of marginalia
I cannot decipher.
They will never help me through this day,
old books like friends too long abandoned.
It is not their fault that time must come.

A fire burns low, mid-afternoon;
the last log jolts to crumble in the grate,
with ashes on my tongue.

In winter woods, the fox is sleeping,
as I walk the fields to see if I can find
what can't be found.

You're not there standing in the husks of corn.
You're not there floating in the black pond water.

Not a whisper in the whitest limbs,
the beautiful appalling grove of trees.

So late to question, but I must insist.

Who knows what happens to the little seeds
that fail to prosper?
Who knows if what is taken by the wind
will ever be returned?

The Lost Scent

Winds off the dumps bring back a childhood
gone, long gone:
the reek of acid-tinged mine water,
smolder of the culm in lowly humps
beside the graveyard
where my father's fathers drift in seams.

I've tried to lose so many things,
too many things,
and now this wind refuses to die down;
it carries in its multiple, gray folds
these whiffs and gleanings
from another life, once all my own.

At School

Warm rain in winter,
and for days the streets
were all awash
in downtown Scranton,
gray snow melting,
sewers overwhelmed.
I went to school without
a hat, without
a thought of what
might follow: flood
or fright, unnatural
disasters. Hours
into dusk I drummed
my fingers on the desk
at school as windows
darkened and the glass
was streaked. My teacher
wept, I don't know why.
I found my mother crying
in the kitchen. I do not
know why. Sometimes
the waters must give way,
the skies tear open,
barrels overflow
and gutters run.

Keyser Valley: 1963

A string of blue lights burning
into dusk: the used cars
huddle, fading as they shine,
a river of debris illumined
by its glower, a wash of dreams.
Some kid in jeans slicks
back his forelock, listens
to a tune: "Love, only love"—
his Chevy plowing
through the tall imagined grain
of what he wants:
the loose-hipped women
he has seen in books, their eyes
like fishhooks, nails
of horn. He slips
through gears, the motions
of his blood, teeth clenched
or grinding. Junkyards
glimmer from the roadway banks,
spare parts, accessories,
a blush of chrome,
bright universal joints,
wire wheels and mirrors.
"Love me every day,"
the hot wind's singing.
"Love me every night."
His engine throttles. Moonlight
drapes the valley with its gown.

To My Father in Late September

A cold sky presses at my window,
and the leaves at every edge go brown.
I watch and listen,
though the walls are thick between us now.
The apples on the tree inside the garden
fall, unpicked. I let them fall
as I must fall and you, my father,
too must fall and sooner
than I'm willing yet to grant.
These blunt successions still appall me:
father into son to dying son,
the crude afflictions of a turning world
that still knows nothing and will never
feel a thing itself, this rock
that's drilled and blasted, cultivated,
left to dry or burn. We soon must learn
its facelessness in sorrow,
learn to touch and turn away,
to settle in the walls of our composure,
and assume a kind of winter knowledge,
wise beyond mere generation
or the ruthless overkill of spring.

The Crow-Mother Tells All

The empty oil drums rattled in the yard
that day in Scranton, and the ham-red hills
would shudder in the distance, thunder-chilled.
My mother shucked a dozen ears of corn,
feeding me stories of the swoop and killings
I could say by heart and still can say.
She hovered in the dust-light, railed
as porch lamps flickered and the power failed,
but not in her. The boom-and-tingle of the storm
was half by her imagined. Hanging on the hard
wings of her apron, always in her sway,
I listened as the green ears all were torn,
her face by lightning cracked and clawed,
her laughter tumbling, beaked and cawed.

The Small Ones Leave Us

The small ones leave us, and the leaves are blown.
It doesn't matter what we do or say,
there's nothing in the end that we can own.

The facts, of course, are all well-known.
We should have understood that come what may
the small ones leave us, and the leaves are blown.

There's nothing in the world that's not on loan:
young children, trees, this house of days.
There's nothing in the end that we can own.

So why regret that each of them has grown?
Why grieve when grasses turn to hay?
The small ones leave us, and the leaves are blown.

This accidental harvest has been sown
and willy-nilly reaped in its own way.
There's nothing in the end that we can own.

What little we can make of skin and bone
unsettles us, who watch and sometimes pray
as small ones leave us and the leaves are blown.
There's nothing in the end that we can own.

New Morning

Light seeps through chinks
as sparrows in the leaves
break out in chatter. Breezes
shift the gauzy curtains,
slip along the wall:
the chill blue fingers
of a northern spring. I let
the blinds up, watching
features I have come to love
spread out before me
like a brassy sea.
I cup your breasts,
the slow warmth of your body
lengthened to my own.
I float upon the surf, the rising
swell of our affection,
driven to the shores
of what we need. Outside,
the world begins without us,
traffic through the lights,
the early news at six o'clock.
The copper river coils
in the sun. It's time, you say,
that you must leave.
Reluctantly, at last,
I let you go, loosen my grip,
let all my kisses turn to air
and lie here by myself
a further hour, thinking
of the way this world

collects us even from ourselves.
My friend, dear bright
incendiary skin,
tomorrow we must love
beyond these boundaries
of day and night,
of wax and wane,
must go on loving even
like the hills that break
beyond New Hampshire into Maine.

Adrift

As night glooms over, slowly
in the bed we rock to sleep,
unmoored, a craft dislodged,
riding the ripples out to sea.
Rain ticks the windows, roof
and walls, a misty drizzle.
Fog comes down
and hovers in the wood
like thinking without words.
We lean into the unspecific
dark, exhausted by the
to-and-fro of accusation.
You said one thing and I
another: neither of us lied,
But language is a wide net cast
at random in the sharpest seas.
The quiver of our catch
is still. We drift now,
tongueless, listing as the rain
sleeks down our house, as
blear November nuzzles us
asleep. We sleep to dream.
We dream to meet the images
that tell and tell again,
to waken into clarity
and names, the speech that
binds us, brings us safely
into dry dock, dawn.

Demonial

They rustle toward you in the dark,
their legions cutting through a mountain trace,
nosing upstream along a bank,
or filing through a basin like red ants,
aware that patience is the way to luck,
the only way to find you in the end.

You can't dissuade them, so give in:
put out some milk or water in a bowl,
a tantalizing morsel that will give them pause.

Pull up a chair, rehearse your speech.
It doesn't matter if, at last, you fail
to ward them off: it's how you greet them,
smiling or with frozen lips and jaw,
your eyes like lightning or a low-watt bulb.

House on Fire

My house on fire in the midday sun
is more than I can watch.
My kindling sons, their fragile bodies,
turn to light.
My wife is lost in auguries of rain.
I take her hand, it turns to wind.
Dry grass is blazing on a windy knob
just out of sight,
as rats take cover in the distant barns.
The woodchucks dig.
The sheep and rocks are huddling in the fields.
My books are curling in the fiery tongues
that want this babble,
that would eat a house so finely cobbled
stone by stone, my house of paper,
flesh and words,
so easily become this fly-ash, bonemeal,
dust of language sucked and blown.

The Ruined House

Deep in the woods, beyond the shuffle
of our works and days, we found a path
between an alley of Norwegian pines.
The children ran on spongy needles,
disappearing in the purple shade;
their shouts were lost among the bird-yip:
tremolo of wood-doves, long diphthong
of redwing blackbirds, crass old crows
all harping on the same old note again.
Your hand in mine, we seemed to drift upon
a fuzzy cumulous of half-voiced thoughts:
the tongue's quick shuttle through the loom of mind
in search of texture, text to sing,
recitativo of a thousand glimpses
caught, composed. All along the way
the eye sought gleanings, images to tell,
to cast one's thoughts on, fix the swell
of meaning in the cross-haired sights
of metaphor, a trope to end all troping:
words and things in pure performance.

Now the hilly path went straightaway ahead,
unfolding with the ease of morning vision.
As they would, the children found it first:
the ruined house on what was once
a breezy hillock in an open field.
The course foundation might have been
a dry stone wall like other walls

now winding over hills, down dingly dells,
to parse the complex sentence of our past,
delineating fields no longer found,
obscured by popple, tamarack and vetch.
The rock foundation of the house in ruins
wasn't stern or morally suggestive.
It had just withstood what it could stand—
the falling stars, the tumbledown of snow,
sharp dislocations of the frosty ground,
the weight of timber soaking in the rain.

We stepped inside behind the children,
who were walking beams like tightrope wires
across a corridor that once led somewhere
warm, familial, and full of light.
The cellar hole was still a hutch of night:
one saw it through the intermittent floorboards
and the two-by-fours exposed like vertebrae
that once held everything in place
but powdered now and sagged toward the middle
as the woodmites fed and moisture softened
grainy fibers, as the mulch of days
began in earnest. There was still a roof
aloft amid the trees, a fragile shade
with patches that were open into sky.
The children clambered up a tilting stairwell
to the second floor; we followed suit,
though not so fearlessly and free
of old conceptions—hurtful images
that hold one back, making one wish
for something less or something more.

The little bedrooms that we found upstairs
were still intact, with built-in beds,
coarse empty shelves still half considering
the weight of objects from their rumored past.
If one stood still and listened close
the voices of the children could be heard,
their laughter in the leaves, the sass and chatter.
Anyway, that's what I told the children,
who believed and listened and could hear.
It's not so hard to frame the past
upon the present, to connect the dots
all still in place, to resurrect and ride
ancestral voices: there is one great tongue.
We find ourselves alive in that old mouth,
through which all meaning flows to sea.
We pour and pour the waters of our lives,
a glittery cascade, its brightness falling
into pools where it must darken once again,
must soak in soil, collect and gather
in a place to tap for future soundings.

Later, in the shade behind the house,
we lingered in the garden's dense enclosure.
Petal-snow of spring once happened there,
the hard ground turned, the stumps uprooted.
Beans and flowers were assigned to rows.
While he would work the upper pasture,
she was left alone sometimes in summer
and would sit there safely in the chestnut shade
to read the Brownings, he and she,
as children napped or slaughtered dragons
with their makeshift swords. That's how the idyll

runs, of course. The typhus and the cold
that cracked the windowpanes in mid-November
and the bitter words: these, too, were true.

We left on hushing feet like thieves
with something in our pockets, awed and fragile.
It was only time that turned those pages,
leaving dust in sunlight on the stairs,
disfiguring the walls that once would keep
a family aloft through hazy fall
and hardy winter into sopping spring.
It was only time that would not stop,
that bore us homeward on the needle path
toward the end of what was ours
a while that summer in the leafy woods.

A Conversation in Oxford

For Isaiah Berlín

Euphonious if not in sync the bells
beat time in amber chapel towers,
and the time has come for tea and talk.
We settle in a room of many shades,
the questions you have spent the decades turning.

"What can we assume about this world?"
you wonder, once again. "What can we claim?"
So little, it would seem. The weak foundations
of all human knowledge make one shudder
to assume too much, to claim too boldly.

"What do you believe?" you ask, so frankly
that I redden, turn, avert my eyes.
"Is consciousness itself an end of foretaste
of a fuller life? This 'oversoul' that Emerson
proposed: Whatever does it mean?"

The honeying facades along the High Street
seem impervious to dwindling light;
whole generations are absorbed
in rheumy passages and darkened cloisters
where so many questions have been put

and left unanswered. It was not a failure
not to answer. I assume that you,
over the decades, have refused to grant

those easy answers that can dull a heart,
occlude a mind, can chain a soul.

You tap your pipe and offer this:
"Real liberty is found in fine gradations,
dartings of the mind—not Big Ideas,
which are mostly preludes to deceit,
embodiments of someone's will-to-power."

I scan the rows of volumes you have filled
with annotations in the well-kept nights—
from Plato to Descartes, from Kant to Kripke.
Herzen was a friend, and Vico, too.
You say that all the best books seize us

half by chance, interrogate and turn us
loose upon ourselves again. I mostly listen,
letting what you say fill up the hour.
The room grows violet and dusky,
insubstantial, as your voice compels

and seems to quicken as your flesh dissolves.
And soon the darkness is itself complete,
consuming everything except your language,
which assumes an Old World gaiety and calm.
I feel, myself, an apparition.

"It is strange," I say. "We find ourselves
alive without a reason, inarticulate
but always trying to re-form a thought
in words that never seem quite right."
I see a flicker in your candle-eyes.

"The world is what it is," you answer strictly,
having seen enough of it to say.
"The world is what you claim it is
as well: this dwindling light, the smoke
of reason, ghostly words in ghostlier air."

I claim this hour, a plum-deep dusk,
the need to pose so many questions,
late, so late—an Oxford afternoon
when everything but language falls away
and words seem all the world we need.

Good Friday in Amalfi

The terrace is a tier of flame tonight,
a lavish send-off to the day,

the red sea curling in the stony cove,
the town lights flickering, a mass of candles

on the dusky shore. Goodbye, I wave,
as long-limbed vines begin to chitter

and the rose-thorns dig, their chafers glinting.
Arum lilies blow their hornlike buds.

Behind my house, the bare-faced cliff
maintains a solitary crooked grin

as if it knows what I have done
or left undone, my desultory sins.

But now it's over, I pretend, near dark,
lifting my arms in racy wind—

white wind that fits me like a loose soutane.
The moon's a wafer dipped in blood.

Signore, I could leave it all tonight.
I could rise—all flutter, whip, and burn.

Still Life

Late afternoon, somewhere in England
by a bowl of apples just past peak,
I could see again: there are no ordinary objects.
Each is lovely in its odd one-offness,
which implies an origin
as strange as mine or yours.
And each is dying in its slow-burn way,
a decomposing that repeats the fall:
a kind of withering bronze sadness
as the skins go dark in different places,
soft and mottled like a baby's scalp,
the fontanel depressed. I could understand
their near disguise in clubby sameness,
and the need to pause in waning sunlight
in a milky bowl. They seek
an equilibrium, a fictive moment
where they feign a freedom from decay
or boring growth. I feel that way
sometimes but lack their classical repose,
the waxy sheen that coddles brightness but allows
a casual release of light,
that sense of safety in small numbers
gathered in a haze, in ripeness
general beyond each shrinking globe,
a fragrance that assembles slowly in the air,
filling up the room with life, still life.

Near Pitlochry

As the sun cut through a cloud,
the hills lit up
like bulbs switched on by unseen hands;
the wind began its spiral climb
from hutch to valley
to the saw-toothed crags where thistle burns.
Alone, in winter,
with my face toward a frost-lit bush,
I waited and was met.

I Was There

I say it, I was there.
No matter what the yellow wind has taken,
I was there, with you.
We have walked out early in the spring
beside the river, when the sun's red shield
was caught in branches
and the bud-tips bled.
We have plucked ripe berries from a hill of brush
in mid-July,
and watched the days go down in flames
in late September,
when the poplar shook its foil.
We have walked on snow in January light:
the long white fields were adamantly bright.
I say it, I was there.
No matter that the evidence is gone,
we heard the honking of the long black geese
and saw them float beyond the town.
Gone all those birds, loose-wristed leaves,
the snowfire, days
we cupped like water in our hands.
So much has slipped through fragile hands.
The evidence is lost, but not these words.
You have my word:
I say it, I was there.

from

Town Life

(1983–1988)

The Mariner

For Richard Kenney

This wide-plank skiff of a table
is rigged for travel,
with a sunny window at my back.
I sit alone here, spinning
an old globe beside my chair, its skin
of colors, planet of my own.
I list the places I would go,
the outer regions of my hands,
the tiny nerve-ends twitching in the night,
the peninsular foot, the nether bowels,
the mucous caverns of my inner ear.
I set my sails each morning after breakfast,
pulling sheets from a left-hand drawer,
taking a pen between my teeth.
The spirits seem to blow
four ways at once or, mostly, not at all.
Even Agamemnon had to slay a daughter
just for winds to carry him to Troy.
I, too, have slaughtered my kin
for motion, for a poem to waste.
Now I spread my charts,
correct my compass, and lay down a course
through the next few hours.
May the gods who brood upon these waters
ease my way, direct the passage
of this fragile craft,
this sloop of self I angle into night.

Syrinx

A summer glebe
at zero noon.
Syrinx—the sound
of pipes across
a weedy pond
unrustles trees.
I wonder if
the sound I think
I heard was real
or not, as in
that wet glade
where Pan discerned
a wilder note
and waded into
water thick
with reeds. That day
he lay as if
unmade against
a moss bank, trying
to recall a note
more overheard
than heard, a sleight
of wind, a sudden
rightness passing
through the world.

The Visitors

Our children sleep among the stars:
blunt, bodiless, unnamed.
The music of their spheres is one long vowel.
None has been signaled from the ground by us,
at least not yet.
Mere argument will never bring them down,
since accidental entry is their mode,
a rupture into flesh,
the starlight overhead past recollection.
Their going will be difficult as well:
a disremembering, consonants disowned.
That change will hurt like every other change.
Only in the spring,
when new grass skims a sudden world,
will any of them understand our need,
our wishing we could hold them,
say their names and set them down.

Differentiation

Already the brow begins to knit,
the arm-buds reach for freedom from the mass,
the eyeholes deepen.

Delicate, the spine uncurls and lengthens,
ganglia and nerve by slow degrees
inhabit what we used to call the soul.

A small pulse separate on its own time,
and none of this is me,
or you, or us.

Brainwaves scatter in the blank of night,
a splay of light from
some new star.

And gently in the amniotic drowse
its face begins to shine,
a lucent stare.

Soon every feature will believe its name,
and tight fists beat across
the broken water.

Crops

And there is sadness in the way they grow—
bell peppers at full gong in mid-July,
the corn breast-high
where mud-prints followed me uphill in May,
loud snapping fingers, peas or beans,
the long-haired chives or rough-tongued mint,
engaging basil,
my fair son,
his tendril body climbing through the air.

History

History has many corridors, yes,
and floodlit stages where the folks
with greater parts than we have
romp, cavort, and trade bold gestures
that affect us all,
and sooty alleys where you'd only go
for love or money;
it's a steeply winding stair,
a sliding board, a tunnel or a ramp,
depending on your gravity of mind
or point of view—but all
the same, the level years
like floors that tumble though a burning house
and come to rest, blue cinders,
on the ground where all things subject
to the laws of change must come to rest,
the shelf of now,
this moment over breakfast
as we touch warm fingers over
toast and jam
and say, okay, I'm glad you're here,
no matter what we said or did before,
I'm glad you're here.

Goodnight, Goodnight

Goodnight, sweet women I have loved

    too little or too late

Bright hair, bright fingernail and bone

      Goodnight, goodnight

On shores of darkness, one by one
the house-lights flicker
as you lay your heads on ice or cloud

    Too near or far

      Goodnight, goodnight

I think of you asleep in far-off cities
with your downy covers drawn up close
a gathering of smells and tastes I've lost

Goodnight, sweet losses

      As the wolves bay shadows on the distant steppes
      as bears eat snow
      as black hawks circle for a place to land
      how far away you seem

your tendrilous pale fingers
kisses, kindnesses
the ill-timed jokes or passing jibes

Forgive me   I forgive

       our tastelessness and ignorance and fear
       our reckless humor, raucous cries

Let each of us, when night falls once for last
rise up and float together, me and you
sucked easily as fly-ash up the flue

In the Sphere of Common Duty

Telemachus did well, I think, to stay,
in spite of what his father might have said
about the promise written in the stars.
The island was all right, nothing fantastic,
but he called it home, then made it home
by taking on himself the fond discharge
of homely duties—taking out the trash,
deciding which of nature's green-leaved things
one should call weeds and separate to mulch,
accepting that it's infinitely harder
to stay put than rush away. Ulysses would have
loved the grand illusion that adventures hang
on precipices, passions, clashing rocks:
the crude near-misses of the manly life;
he went off to war, as men still do,
for reasons the community allowed
were just and not just his. But once the Trojans
had been done to death: What then? What then?
"Boys will be boys," they always say.
Think of him, Telemachus, who loved the stars
no less for watching them from where he stood.

Reading Through the Night

Late reading, and our books dissolve
in thunder, lightning through the rain;
their lights burn single in the mind.

Your novel and my novel move together,
line by line, like Noah's animals,
who found the ark, each other as the flood-

tide rose. Our oaky bed, its headboard
of a prow, lifts over waves. Your hero
and my heroine engage, as night whelms over

and the one great plot, that salty stew,
as ever, thickens. In a single sheet, we feel
the rise and fall of breath, the generations

that have come and gone and come again.
Is nothing ever lost? Eternal climax,
denouement: we find ourselves, at dawn,

on that bare hillside, disembarked,
the animals afoot, our novels turning
on themselves again, their separate spines.

Skiing Home at Dusk

This is the blessed hour when shadows lengthen
on the blue-red snow, when skiers mount
the billows with an ease, a forward *shush*,

and memory excites the tilt toward home:
the woody fire that blossoms over logs,
the candle and the book, hibernal harvest.

Motion through the trees collects the soul,
a whispering in transit, wind that's caught
like music in the flute's brief wooden throat.

This is the hour of accepted grace,
when everywhere we've been comes down to this:
the edge of day, where particles of thought

cohere like atoms in a structured dance
around one center that we call ourselves,
like poetry: the patterned perfect dance

of sentences that rise and fall with sense,
a language adequate to what we see
and feel and hear, a broad equivalence,

the center of the mind as clear as winter
with its empty backlit bedrock sky,
the motes of snow-dust blowing in the trees.

This is the hour when skiers and their skis
make one crisp sound, when every object
revels in its name, when *home* is home.

Town Life

For Ann Beattie

It strikes me as the best of every world
this morning as I leave the house at nine
and walk uptown, past shuttered houses
I have learned by heart down to the angle
of each sloping roof, all kinds of siding
and their various degrees of disrepair.
I've memorized the shrubbery and lawns,
with each reflective of their owners' minds,
the blend of trees, some planted by the town
in 1920, others here by chance,
a drift of wind, or someone's purpose.
Today September-blooming mountain laurels
burn with flowers to fill the gaps where long-
necked elms once made a tunnel of their leaves.
I know this sidewalk as a blind man knows
his way around his house: the tilting flagstones
and the gravel drives, macadam stretches
that will heave with frost by mid-December.
And my joints adjust to ups and downs
as I proceed, half drunk on air, on night-
rinsed grasses and the gilt-edged leaves
that riffle in the slightest wind with that
low rustling tinny note of early fall,
a note of loss that makes me savor
what befalls each step: the wedge of geese
that arrows overhead between slate roofs,
the exoskeletons of huge black ants
that file like soldiers through the Khyber Pass
to certain failure in the winter's grip,

the squirrels rippling in gray blurs up trees
with preservations in their iron jaws.

There's so much going on I'll never know
but happily assume has its own pattern;
I have mine, which fits into the town's
slow ritual so well no doubt you'll wonder
if some parts of me were not lopped off
to make this fitting. Wouldn't I prefer
to wake at dawn in country heaven, acres
of raw land around my house, with crops to tend
and cows dew-lapping through the shallow swales?
Some friends cut wood to save their souls
while I burn oil; they hike into the hills
for rustic solace as I walk these streets.
I've other friends who live in cities and believe
in motion multiplied by will, the swirl
of faces, calendars with no blank spaces left.
Their lives are verticals of glass and steel.
I don't begrudge them what they've found to work.
I'm all for anything that makes you feel
the gravity afoot, the tug of light
particulars, the sway of chosen hours,
though I love town life and its appointments
of well-paced events, the tower that chimes,
life in concentric circles that acknowledge
morning, noon, and night, the falling seasons
that enforce their rules, make us accede
to larger motions than we make ourselves.
I love the neighboring of little towns,
the expectations that are often met
by characters we greet with friendly nods:
the waitress at the diner where I drink

my de-caf coffee, one old cop who never
says hello, too charged with duty to descend
to pleasantries on county time, the dozen
keepers of the dozen shops who fill my life
with necessary objects, food, and service.
Their worlds depend upon my morning walk,
my needs and whims. And so we live in
symbolic swirl around the center
of the village green: its white gazebo
like a hub of sorts, the centrifugal
aim of all our motion, though it's really
useless as a building goes, except for
concerts by the local bands on summer nights.
That white gazebo is the town's real heart:
a minor symbol of nostalgic longing
for our fictive past amid the hubbub
of our daily work in buildings shaped
to useful ends: the Greco-Roman banks
with much more cash than anybody needs
to make one life, the small post office
that can ship our mail to Bognor Regis
or Addis Ababa without any hitch.
It seems that we can eat our cake and have it,
although wisdom votes against that thought.
I use the royal "we" perhaps too glibly,
since I'll never stand for public office
or consent to join the Rotary or Elk.
(My love of town life doesn't go that far.)
Whatever else I do, I'll fill these streets
with all the shambling presence I can muster
for enough good years to say I've been here
and have met them well on equal terms.
I'll be one spoke in this bright wheel

that spins through decades at its chosen speed,
that passing airplanes notice like a dime
in heavy grass—a glint of silver—
something they would probably pick up
if only it were not so far away.

Suburban Swamp

The swamp at the end of our cozy county road
does nothing for the value of what we own;
it's what the agents call an eyesore
and the neighbors never mention to their friends,
half-wishing what they never set in words
will not exist. I'm standing by the stumps
that fizzle like antacid tabs in water,
the tatty oaks too old for leaves, loose
at the roots like blackened teeth that wobble
in the gums, a periodontal nightmare.
This was once a lake, old-timers say,
remembering the sunny Sunday picnics
where these moss banks grow or, some say,
"fester." Frogs exhale into the midday air.
The green-gold water pops its blisters.
Winds are redolent of larval scum
that might well be a soothing balm for backache
in an old wives' tale if old wives lived.
The Indians came out in bark canoes
two centuries ago; now Boy Scouts tramp
the margins for a merit badge or two,
birdwatchers wait for oddly feathered friends,
and secret moralists inspect the setting
for its sheer decay. I like it how
what happens happens out of sight here.
Business goes on beneath the surface.
Transformations: water into froth,
great hulking logs to pulp and steam.
Here every change is hidden but complete,
all purposes obscured—a skilled dismantling,
de-creation into light and air.

The Function of Winter

I'm for it, as the last leaves shred
or powder on the floor, as sparrows find
the driest footing, and November rains
fall hard as salt sprayed over roads.
The circulating spores take cover
where they can, and light runs level
to the ground again: no more the vertical
blond summer sheen that occupies a day,
but winter flatness—light as part of things,
not things themselves. My heart's in storage
for the six-month siege we're in for here,
laid up for use a little at a time
like hardtack on a polar expedition,
coveted though stale. Ideas, which in
summer hung a crazy jungle in my head,
subside now, separate and gleam in parts;
I braid them for display on winter walls
like garlic tails or onions, crisp bay wreaths.
One by one, I'll pluck them into spring.
If truth be told, I find it easier
to live this way: the fructifying boom
of summer over, wild birds gone, and wind
along the ground where cuffs can feel it.
Everything's in reach or neatly labeled
on my basement shelves. I'm ready to begin
to see what happened when my heart was hot,
my head too dazzled by itself to think.

A Lost Topography

Starfall, backfill—
home again: the headlamps flicker on the dumps,
the backhoes leveling
the once-bright culm that filled the air
with reek of memory, the red-
blue hills of April dusk,
when I would walk this way from school,
imagining the lives plowed under, lost,
the phosphorescent names
like Nanticoke or Pittston, Moosic or Old Forge.
If only I could count the stars that fell here,
fell and cooled,
resumed a lusterless composure
on this sandy field, a rich moraine
where moonwort thrives,
where thistle and white mold
become an overlay, where substance
crumbles and the pigeons gloom.

Passing Through Vermont on Three Martinis

For purple miles the mountains rise
above the river. Barns
assemble in surrounding corn.
The traveler takes nothing here for granted,
tippling under ice-and-vodka skies.
He listens to the water's racy babble
and discerns a meaning. Even
when the wind yanks back a shutter,
he perceives a sign. A farm boy
fishing in the distance moves him
more than a museum. Cowbells
tinkle in the distant calm.
He vows to quit his salaried position
one fine day, returning to this spot
to sip forever as the mountains rise.

America

How could I forget you, with your peaks
like compound fractures poking through the skin,
your svelte, deciduously fluttering trees
and conifers that bristle, jacked with light
on chilly slopes: blue western mountains
I have flown above but never hiked?
How could I ignore your gainly rivers—
Merrimack and Hudson, Mississippi,
with their slender reefs and ox-bow turns,
Ohio, Delaware, and Susquehanna—
on and on, running with grandiloquent
profusion through the grassy lands? They seem
restrained, for all their grandeur, and as if
they understood their place in commerce even more
than nature and would not obstruct the flow
of goods, unlike unruly counterparts elsewhere:
the Ganges or the Nile, who regularly
drown whole populations, or the useless Congo,
pouring through a smoke of stinging flies,
or the Thames and Seine, content to lie
forever in repose reflecting spires,
flying buttresses, and gargoyle faces
that inspire a nation to adore its past
more than its future, unlike you,
who never gave a whit for history except
as something you could sell as pretty tours
in Williamsburg or Boston—legendary homes
with brassy plaques and monumental stares.
You were always one to yearn toward,
excited by the thought of pure production,

freedom to expand, revise old parts,
create a mall where mills once rattled
through their ten-hour shifts, transform
a dingy tenement to flat and quaint
boutiques, unfazed by barriers of brick
or finance. You advance by instinct, gifted
with a swift, revisionary mind that won't
let go. I know you by your restlessness
and brooding: smokestacks smudging up the sky,
the ten-lane highways that converge and tangle
in spaghetti loops, the open roads
that make a desert one more backdrop
as the trucks roll by, the buses, cars.
You're driven by a glad and giddy heart
that's open to the world and wants the world
to imitate your broad, successful gestures
and be rich as you are, clean and free.
All poverty and weakness hide their eyes
in your hard glare, are driven into corners,
left to mourn or fester out of sight.
I'd know you anywhere, my dashing country,
who can never say *enough*, who watches me
like Mom, believing that my fate is yours
as well. You let me breathe you and become
your body, linger in your arms, or leave you
for another, far-off country, where
the customs differ and your name is mud.
But then you welcome me, a rebel son
come home again to join the work at hand,
this fond production that becomes a story
you will never read but cherish nonetheless.

Portrait of the Artist as an Old Man

In Vermont, 2038

In the dark glass, forward, the abysmal time
    to come, you read your visage
        in memorial mind,
     a broad-domed squire
leaning on a cane, a wide-brimmed hat

pulled rakishly across a sun-burned patch
    of flaking skin, a brow
         whose clench
    betrays impatience with a world
abandoned to its foolish self so many times.

At sunset, at great height, you watch the hawk
    scythe down the shadows
      of another day,
    admiring how it hangs there,
steady in the wind that whets its wings.

You think of Thomas Hardy, Yeats and Graves—
    the grand old men—of dear
      Red Warren,
    friend and mentor, whom you loved
to love, or Frost: Old Rocky Face himself.

I'm one of them, you say, and hope, lips smacking,
    drooling, one might say, still
      recomposing
    in your heart a life you've since
revised ten thousand times, no version

truer than the one before, or so it seems.
    Oh, how can you forget
        so many facts,
    the petty hatreds, fears, the fond
betrayals, posturings, reprisals—worse?

Maybe nothing matters but the final gloss,
    that beautifully wrought,
        penultimate
    revision made before the dark
blots every word, and heaven, like a blank page,

shines pristinely but, unlike before,
    needs no embossing, none of this
        black print
    you think adds something
to a paltry silence you cannot endure.

On midnight's mountain, in a cloak of stars,
    you look for answers to
        strong questions
    posed, a little falsely, re-
composed each day like shopping lists or prayers.

Will you ever know if any of those guises—
    hawk or mole, the fox,
        sweet ingénue,
    the rake or fool, the wise old man—
meant anything beyond their deft performance?

Will anyone replace the shattered hours,
    those pitiable shards which,
        reassembled
    in the bright Beyond, might
constitute, at last, a kind of heaven?

Portrait of the Artist Underground

In 2063

The roots become him, in their timeless thrall,
    the delicate and wormlike
        shoots of green
    that seem to bind him but which
set him free, loose through the ground.

He has no more need of calculation,
    love or money, even
        paltry things
    like bread or water; he has all
he wants of endlessly recurring lotus-silence,

which he takes for song, of dark and light,
    the lavish shadows, suns
        that drill the rock
    and liberate the vapor soul,
whatever in the last completes his shining.

He is past redemption, past regret
    for petty misdemeanors,
        crimes of passion,
    civilized commitments to
those guises which conceal the hungry heart.

His heart is left with only what it loved,
    and loved entirely,
        woman in
    one name, the beautiful
redoublings, words he gardened into silence,

which was his last shrine, his Bo tree, blooming
in the soil today, its
petal flowers
flimsy and delicious on
his lips and eyelids, palms, the dirt, the wetness

that confirms this world, that speaks for everything
now quick and running, while
he lords it
over, in the Lord-won air,
all men and women in the selfsame stare.

Divine Parameters

The gull floats into the sun and flares,
a spray of sparks.

                            The wind says nothing.

Now you understand time's only end,
with distance as the way from here to there,
a leap across the dark from fire to fire.

Solstice, Entering Capricorn

In distant states, the snow is falling
over silent fields that hide
the missiles, blue deer

running in the frozen woods behind the wind,
the winter apples black as figs,
choke cherries buried

in the plates of ice beyond recall.
In submarines, off shore, sub-zero weather,
warheads sleep

like prehistoric fish with one eye open.
Hammerheads move slowly through the depths;
the minnows darken.

Wolves tug firmly on their leash of sound
in Russian steppes
as bombers wait in icy hangars,

pilots shiver through the dreamless sleep
of those on call.
The black crows gather overhead in minds

of mice and rabbits. Spinning
in an ether all its own,
the earth knows nothing of its slow disease

as Capricorn, the goat-horn, digs
for spring, unable to contain its forward
tilt, its ignorant religion.

This Kampuchea

We sit in a *tuk-tuk* with binoculars,
sipping Fantas, as a hot white wind
blows over water half a mile wide—
a heat that most of us can just abide.
Pale tourists, young voyeurs: we find
humidity a subject. Kids with scars

across their cheeks and narrow backs beg
candies, cigarettes. We give them coins
that mean so little we can hardly not afford
to give them up. Such charity! I pour
my Fanta in a cup and give a swig
to a small boy whose mother joins

us from behind a shack, an improvised
bamboo construction housing refugees.
She hasn't said a word since she escaped,
the doctor tells us. Maybe she was raped
at knifepoint, maybe she had seen the trees
strung out with villagers Pol Pot despised

for simply being there. Then we all hear
they shot her husband in a ditch before her eyes;
her eyes seem blank now, darkly blank.
I notice that she never seems to blink
but watches like a bald-eyed moon, in fear,
as children utter their unlovely cries

for candy, cigarettes, for sips of Fanta
from my tinny cup. The bamboo clicks
in big-finned leaves across the river where
Cambodia has turned in its despair
to Kampuchea, where the golden bricks
of Angkor Wat sink like Atlantis

into jungle depths, the lost bright heart
of ancient quietude that's since been drowned
in spit and blood. I wonder why we came
to this sad border and if we're to blame
as much as anyone in that swart
jungle where the millions died as Death found

easy entrance on the world, engorged
itself, while faces turned another way.
Lon Nol, Pol Pot, the bloated Princes
whom the Rouge detested: none convinces
us that he's to blame. We'll never say
"this one" or "that" and feel relieved, purged

and guiltless, free to sail by 747
home to seasons in the hills of ease.
This Kampuchea has become a tomb
inside me, alien, but still a home
in some strange way—an altar where my knees
will fall at intervals, an odd chance given

to me as a gift, a place to bow
in obeisance to the darkest gods
who rule the heart whenever we ignore
our greatest charge: to watch and pray. The shore-
line glistens as a boy lets down a bamboo
rod, an old man settles by a tree and nods

off into dreams, a flame-bright bird
sails over water without any sense
of human borders. Children scurry to a jeep
beside us where the spoils are greater, as we keep
to schedule and drive away: untold expense
now memorized as what we saw and heard.

At the Ice Cream Parlor

Maybe it doesn't matter, but this chair—
black curlicues of iron, ice cream-parlor
perfect with its plastic seat and legs
right out of Paris in the Gilded Age—
reminds me of the one and only chair
that Plato dreamed of in his abstract heaven,
lofty and original and pure,
where every single noun is past declension,
where all men are Man, and Wolf is feral
to the nth degree, where Oak knows nothing
of November's claim upon its leaves,
its dainty little hands aquiver in
a blue, long-winded Breeze at noon forever,
while the Brook runs by with saucy stories
of the life upriver lively on its tongue,
as if bright gossip were the only end
of light and water, pebbles and white sand.
So all these things set out before me—
peppercorns and napkins, spoons, white bowls—
exist as versions of their final selves
(refracted in the dark receding mirrors,
a *mise-en-abîme* of checkered tablecloths
and sundry guests with lavish sundaes),
and each new spoon or peppercorn or bowl
or whatnot idles in its mere potential,
wondering if any bold recension
will effect the change to end all change.

Yet I sometimes wonder if we have the right
to postulate an ultimate revision
of each blessed thing, ignoring how

each object seems quite settled in its way,
not obviously hoping to progress
to some new state. One might as well propose
that everything delights in what it is,
its thingy presence, or at least accepts
what has been given and ignores our pompous,
motherly demand for something more.
Duns Scotus was, of course, appalled
that finer objects in the world's demesne
should have to be subjected to such pressure;
we ought to understand that sheer discreteness
is a good itself, the great sage thought,
conceiving of a neatly fretted world
where each leaf shimmers on each separate tree
without regard to anyone's conception
of a Tree or Leaf, each discontinuously
blazing forth like these black chairs, these bowls
and peppercorns and napkins, plastic spoons.
I probably would like a world like that,
where pebbles in the local gargling brook
aspired to nothing but their gargling selves,
where every flower was its own condition,
brittle and as bright as day could manage
but no more or less, and where each creature
was a thing apart, an entity composed
yet still composing, with successive states
discretely happy without longing toward
some final version in some perfect sky.

That notion of creation satisfies
our need to love what's here, to value time's
sweet local nimbus as a holy thing,
but only for a while. We begin too soon

to long for something we can barely scry,
to read for essences in what's been given
and resent the sense of time as present
and not past as well, the loss of future
as a light toward which all things grow.

The self that I admit each day in passing
(if I may divert this to myself)
is a paltry fellow, prone to narrowness
and self-regard, unwilling to add
charity most times to faith and hope,
and even faith has mostly to go begging
in a little heart that can't expand
without exception and which rarely opens
to the world at large. The self I live with
is too mean to show, so lives disguised
in raiments of good fellowship and niceness,
decency and truth. He's proudly crafty
in the way he works, a fond dissembler
who has done more harm than anyone
would guess who didn't know, though I dismiss
him in my better moments and go off alone,
imagining that vision in my head
of his Big Brother up in Plato's sky,
a sort of guardian or souped-up angel
who regards me fondly from afar
and faintly through the milky glass of heaven
offers me a glimmer of fresh hope,
a finer version of the self I show,
a last recension I may only know
by lofting thither some appointed day.

Right now, I'm happy to believe that once
released from guilt and pressures to conform
or change my mind, free of all petty notions
of position, pride, or valor, I'll find myself
at peace beside all others in their final draft,
the absolute in hand that I have glimpsed
in offhand moments in unlikely places
(such as this dim parlor with its ice cream
chairs and tacky tables and recessive mirrors
that track a semblance of the man I am).
I'm happy to believe that every object
may well have a chance to change its name,
to clarify its essence and become
more like itself than nature will allow
in these rough drafts, these early versions
of that fabled state, the life to come.

Grandmother in Heaven

In a plume-field, white above the blue,
she's pulling up a hoard of root crops
planted in a former life and left to ripen:
soft gold carrots, beets, bright gourds.
There's coffee in the wind, tobacco smoke
and garlic, olive oil and lemon.
Fires burn coolly through the day,
the water boils at zero heat.
It's always almost time for Sunday dinner,
with the boys all home: dark Nello,
who became his cancer and refused to breathe;
her little Gino, who went down the mines
and whom they had to dig all week to find;
that willow, Tony, who became so thin
he blew away; then Julius and Leo,
who survived the others by their wits alone
but found no reason, after all was said,
for hanging on. They'll take their places
in the sun today at her high table,
as the antique beams light up the plates,
the faces that have lately come to shine.

At the Ruined Monastery in Amalfi

For Charles Wright

On a hill, approaching Easter,
well above the sea's bland repetitions
of the same old story
and the town's impenitent composure,
I survey old grounds.

The fire-winged gulls ungulf the tower.
Lesser grackles, nuns and tourists,
scatter on the grass.

The brandy-colored light of afternoon
seeps through the stonework;
creeping flowers buzz and flutter
in the limestone cracks.

Wisteria-chocked loggias drip with sun.

A honeycomb of cells absorbs the absence
it has learned to savor;
court and cloister close on silence,
the auroral prayers long since burned off
like morning fog.

The business of eternity goes on behind our backs.

In the chapel dark,
I'm trying to make out a worn inscription

on a wind-smudged altar,
but the Latin hieroglyphs have lost their edge.

Remember me, *Signore*,
who has not yet learned to read your hand,
its alphabet of buzz and drip and flutter.

from

Anthracite Country

(1975–1982)

The Sabine Farm

You spoke of Horace on his Sabine farm,
his lime-deep valley, hyacinth in bloom,
with holm oak forests shuffling in the breeze.
He loved the spring, the clover-laden grass
his herds would feed on, drizzle-sweetened hills.
He lived, well free of Rome, as if the world
were leafy and reposed, the weekly gossip
flowing from the courts Augustus kept:
a gabbling stream of anecdote, opinion,
downright lies. Through confident, warm years,
with kingly patrons tending to his needs,
he dug the furrows of his perfect odes.

I know a few of us would surely prize
that farm: soft fontanel of private earth
in which to plow the furrows of our verse,
to separate the tangled roots of speech,
possess the ground, the poet's measured tongue.
A few of us would love that greening world
with boundaries to walk and contemplate:
the pastures of desire, unweeded, blown
by riffles of blue wind; unforded brooks
of memory and dream; the icy cliffs
where waterfalls of purpose pour their vowels
through steady air, a music we could learn.

My friend, we follow in the Roman colter's
wake in our own ways, not really farmers,
but poachers on the farm Maecenas granted.
Now weekly gossip flows along the wires

from Boston to Vermont; the capital's
alive, but Caesars in their private jets
want nothing of us now. The mailman comes
with letters to aggrieve us, forms to fill.
I pay my debts, as you do, with a shrug
and turn to cultivate the ground, protected
by the barbed-wire fencing of our prose.
Unpatronized, we groom this inward land.

Beginning the World

The crossing from sleep to waking
was easy those early winter mornings
when the snow fell dumb and bright as stars.

My mother packed me to the nose
in scarves; she tied a hat to my head
and sent me stumbling in boots through hills of snow.

The way was a desert of white,
dunes whirling in the streets where cars
lay buried, humped and sleeping like camels.

And I loved that whiteness,
the unyielding blankness of it all
that left me alone with the whole world unimagined.

Today, marooned by decades
and distance from those days and winters,
I close my eyes to begin the world again.

Walking the Trestle

They are all behind you, grinning,
with their eyes like dollars, their shouts
of *dare you, dare you, dare you*
broken by the wind. You squint ahead
where the rusty trestle wavers into sky
like a pirate's plank. And sun shines
darkly on the Susquehanna, forty feet
below. You stretch your arms
to the sides of space and walk
like a groom down that bare aisle.
Out in the middle, you turn to wave
and see their faces breaking like bubbles,
the waves beneath you flashing coins,
and all around you, chittering cables,
birds, and the bright air clapping.

Playing in the Mines

Never go down there, fathers told you,
over and over. The hexing cross
nailed onto the door read DANGER, DANGER.
But playing in the mines once every summer,
you ignored the warnings. The door
swung easier than you wished; the sunlight
followed you down the shaft a decent way.
No one behind you, not looking back,
you followed the sooty smell of coal dust,
close damp walls with a thousand facets,
the vaulted ceiling with its crust of bats,
till the tunnel narrowed, and you came
to a point where the playing stopped.
You heard old voices pleading in the rocks;
they were all your fathers, longing to fix you
under their gaze and to go back with you.
But you said to them NEVER, NEVER
as a chilly bile washed round your ankles.
You stood there wailing your own black fear.

1913

"Guarda, Ida, la còsta!"
She imagined, as she had for weeks,
a dun shore breaking through the fog,
a stand of larkspur, houses
on the curling bay.

As wind broke over the gunwales,
a fine low humming.

It was sudden when she came
to rest, the *Santa Vincenta*, thudding
into dock. The tar-faced lackeys
lowered the chains, seals
popped open, and the ship disgorged
its spindly crates, dark trunks
and children with their weepy frowns.
There were goats and chickens,
litters and a score of coffins
on the wharf at once.

Cold, wet, standing by herself
in the lines of custom
under some grey dome, rain falling
through the broken glass above her,
she could think of nothing
but the hills she knew:
the copper grasses, olives
dropping in the dirt, furze
with its yellow tongues of flower.

The Missionary Visits Our Church
in Scranton

He came to us every other summer
from the jungles of Brazil,
his gabardine suit gone shiny in the knees
from so much praying.

He came on the hottest Sunday, mid-July,
holding up a spear before our eyes,
the very instrument, we were told,
which impaled a brace of his Baptist colleagues.

The congregation wheezed in unison,
waiting for the slides: the savage women
dandling their breasts on tawny knees,
the men with painted buttocks
dancing in a ring.

The congregation loosened their collars,
mopped their brows, all praying
that the Lord would intervene.

Always, at the end, one saw the chapel:
its white-baked walls, the circle of women
in makeshift bras, the men in shirts.

They were said to be singing a song of Zion.
They were said to be wishing us well in Scranton.

The Miner's Wake

In memoriam: E.P.

The small ones squirmed in suits and dresses,
wrapped their rosaries round the chair legs,
tapped the walls with squeaky shoes.

But their widowed mother, at thirty-four,
had mastered every pose of mourning,
plodding the sadness like an ox through mud.

Her mind ran well ahead of her heart,
making calculations of the years without him
that stretched before her like a humid summer.

The walnut coffin honeyed in sunlight;
calla lilies bloomed over silk and satin.
Nuns cried heaven into their hands

while I, a nephew with my lesser grief,
sat by a window, watching pigeons
settle onto slag like summer snow.

Coal Train

Three times a night it woke you
in middle summer, the Erie Lackawanna,
running to the north on thin, loud rails.
You could hear it coming a long way off:
at first, a tremble in your belly,
a wire trilling in your veins, then diesel
rising to a froth beneath your skin.
You could see the cowcatcher,
wide as a mouth and eating ties,
the headlight blowing a dust of flies.
There was no way to stop it.
You lay there, fastened to the tracks
and waiting, breathing like a bull,
your fingers lit at the tips like matches.
You waited for the thunder of wheel and bone,
the axles sparking, fire in your spine.
Each passing was a kind of death,
the whistle dwindling to a ghost in air,
the engine losing itself in trees.
In a while, your heart was the loudest thing,
your bed was a pool of night.

Tanya

One day after school
I was running the tracks
back into the country
in early spring, sunlight
glazing the chips of coal,
old bottles and beer cans
shoaling the sides. I ran
for miles, stripped
to the belly, dogwood
odors in the air like song.

When I stopped for breath
I saw there were women
bending in the ferns.
They spoke in Polish,
their scarlet dresses
scraping the ground
as they combed for mushrooms,
plucking from the grass
blond spongy heads
and filing their pouches.

But the youngest one
danced to herself in silence.
She was blond as sunlight
blowing in the pines.
I whispered to her... *Tanya*.
She came when the others
moved away, and she gave me
mushrooms, touching my cheek.

I kissed her forehead:
it was damp and burning.

I found myself sprinting
the whole way home
with her bag of mushrooms.
The blue sky rang
like an anvil stung
with birds, as I ran
for a thousand miles to Poland
and further east, to see her
dancing, her red skirt
wheeled in the Slavic sun.

Snake Hill

The dirt road rose abruptly through a wood
just west of Scranton, strewn by rusty wire,
abandoned chassis, bottles, bits of food.

We used to go there with our girls, those nights
in summer when the air like cellophane
stuck to your skin, scaling the frenzied heights

of teenage lust. The pebbles broke like sparks
beneath our tires; we raised an oily dust.
The headlights flickered skunk-eyes in the dark.

That way along the hill's illumined crown
was Jacob's ladder into heaven; cars
of lovers, angel-bright, drove up and down.

There was a quarry at the top, one strip
worked out, its cold jaws open, empty-mouthed.
A dozen cars could park there, hip to hip.

There I took Sally Jarvis, though we sat
for six hours talking politics. I was
Republican, and she was Democrat.

We talked our way through passion, holding hands;
the moon, gone egg-yolk yellow in the sky,
tugged firmly at our adolescent glands.

I kissed her once or twice, far too polite
to make a rude suggestion, while the stars
burned separately, hard as anthracite.

The city was a distant, pinkish yawn
behind our backs as we leant head to head.
The dead-end quarry held us there till dawn.

Working the Face

On his belly with a coal pick
mining underground:
the pay was better for one man
working the face.
Only one at a time could get
so close, his nose
to the anthracite, funneling
light from a helmet, chipping
with his eyes like points of fire.
He worked, a taproot
tunneling inward, layer
by layer, digging
in a world of shadows,
thick as a slug against the floor,
dark all day long.
Wherever he turned, the facets
showered a million stars.
He was prince of darkness,
stalking the village at 6 P.M.,
having been to the end of it,
core and pith
of the world's rock belly.

The Lackawanna at Dusk

Here is a river lost to nature,
running in its dead canal
across the county, scumming its banks.
I lean out over the water,
poking my head through rusty lace
of the old rail bridge and blowing
my spits out into its swill.
A slow wind ushers the homely smell
around my head; I breathe its fumes.
In whirlpool eddies, odds
of garbage and poisoned fish
inherit the last red hour of light.
A ripe moon cobbles the waters.
Mounds of culm burn softly into night.

Anthracite Country

The culm dump burns all night,
unnaturally blue, and well below heaven.
It smolders like moments almost forgotten,
the time when you said what you meant
too plainly and ruined your chance of love.

Refusing to dwindle, fed from within
like men rejected for nothing specific,
it lingers at the edge of town, unwatched
by anyone living near. The smell now
passes for nature. It would be missed.

Rich earth-wound, glimmering
rubble of an age when men
dug marrow from the land's dark spine,
it resists all healing.
Its luminous hump cries comfortable pain.

The Rain School

I entered the rain school, mud and water—
where the words were almost sensings, splashed,
a sibilant cool stream—that summer
when the river's tongue grew thick and frothy
and the town afraid. The city fathers

gathered on the banks to watch it brim,
the Lackawanna feeding on itself.
The women closed in circles of despair,
imagining a planet dowsed and drowned,
a biblical demise. I gorged my ankles,

trekking by myself, a slop of steps
through silt that left no open-ended vowels,
a vanished printing. Wading, I was
far out, plunging in the mud,
the subsoil gouged and healing underneath.

The Salt Lick

I found this jawbone relic of a deer.
The brook beside it gargled in the strait,
a narrow rapids, something of a ford.
White foam and algae lathered where the hinge
once bit for apples, licked for salt.

An arrow in its side, perhaps a bullet,
this is where it fell. The hunter
never followed in its tracks. And here
it settled into hard, cold sleep
having lost the will to stumble farther on.

One night I dug its body to restore it:
set the hazel jelly of its gaze,
refilled the silken pouches of its lungs
and stretched new hide. It wakened into air!
I watched it loping to its thicket lair.

Learning to Swim

That summer in Tunkhannock the cold stream
barked, dogs herding over stones. Behind me,
wading with a switch of willow in your hand,
you drove me out: large father
with your balding, sun-ripe head, quicksilver

smiles. I wavered over pebbles,
small, white curds, and listened into fear:
the falls that sheared the stream close by,
the gargle and the basalt boom.
"It's safe," you said. "Now go ahead and swim."

I let it go, dry-throated, lunging.
Currents swaddled me from every side,
my vision reeling through the upturned sky.
Half dazed and flailing in a whelm of cries,
I felt your big hand father me ashore.

Berry-Picking

In July the huckleberries ripened.
Bushes swarmed with honeybees and wasps.
We worked in pairs, first scouting
from a bluff for clustered crops. I filled
my pail, my fingers gashed and bloody with the juice.

In corners where the rest would never guess
we'd gone, I gave you fistfuls,
berries from my hoard. Our stomachs swelled;
the black juice stained the innocence of smiles.
We lay on moss banks thick as suede.

I told you that your lips were Beaujolais,
unsure of what I meant. You stroked my chin
and swore to wear the letters of my school.
Our friends would never see us as we were:
my hands, the rose-blown color of your teats.

The Sea Lily

I found it on a culm bank near Old Forge:
the fossil of an ancient crawler
printed firmly in a slab of coal.
I took it home, the image of its delicate
horned shell and pincer-claws.

That summer in my bedroom, late one night,
I woke: a green moon eerily aflame
had caught the fossil in its funnel-light.
The creature shone, its eyes
were globed fruit swaying on their stems.

Last night I saw it shining in a dream,
the cilia on fire. Unnerved, I fossicked
in a book to find its name,
a miner in the word-bank, digger
in the tongue's lost gleaming quarry.

Amores (After Ovid)

An afternoon in sultry summer.
After swimming, I lay on the long divan,
dreaming of a tall brown girl.

Nearby, a din of waves
blasted in the jaws of rocks.
The green sea wrestled with itself
like a muscular beast in the white sun.

A tinkle of glasses woke me: Corinna!
She entered with fruit and wine.
I remember the motion of her hair
like seaweed across her shoulders.

Her dress: a green garment.
She wore it after swimming.
It pressed to the hollows of her body
and was beautiful as skin.

I tugged at the fringe, politely.
She poured out wine to drink.
"Shy thing," I whispered.

She held the silence with her breath,
her eyes to the floor, pretending,
then smiling: a self-betrayal.

In a moment she was naked.
I pulled her down beside me,
lively, shaking like an eel—

loose-limbed and slippery-skinned.
She wriggled in my arms at play.

When I kissed her closer
she was wet beneath me and wide as the sea.

I could think of nothing but the sun,
how it warmed my spine as
I hugged her, shuddering all white light,
white thighs. Need more be said

but that we slept as if
the world had died together with that day?

These afternoons are rare.

In the Meadow

Old Guernseys hover in the sun,
their brown sides hung from nape
to tailbone, a two-pole tent,
their legs like switches. Walking

in the meadow, we step over dung:
the dry flat discs, some wet with midges.
Daisies sputter in the heat
as we lie down, the milkweed crushing

beneath our backs its creamy stems.
We shiver in our skins.
Who looks beyond us, tangled, feeling
for what we are, looks too far.

Seasons of the Skin

The beginning was hills, moss-covered stones,
October flowers. I climbed all day,
those damp beginnings. I felt
your arms like roots around me, love
like burdocks clinging to my legs;
the trees cried nothing but wind.

Winter was a crop of bones.
I remember your valley rimed with frost,
the slippery ledges, branches under snow.
I saw that your eyes were ponds of love
locked over with ice. I pecked
for a season into that gaze.

The spring was running. Icicles,
glazed by sunlight, narrowed to a drip,
and the moon shot awkward glances.
A nub of crocus started from your belly;
there was water spinning over stones.
I listened in the green-leaved world.

Then a jay flipped over the pines,
a blue tail flashing. Sunlight
sharpened its edges on the rocks,
and feathery bracken softened your body.
I drew upon you in the heated grass
to see that your eyes were open water.

Swimming in Late September

We listen:
the hush of apples falling through a dark,
the crackling of pines.
A slow wind circles the pond
like an ancient bird with leathery wings.

I float, my belly to the moon,
lifting my toes through cold, black water.
You brush against me, fanning your hair,
so close we are touching head to foot.

Frog-eyes sparkle in the ferns
as if they wonder
who would be swimming in late September.
Already the crickets have lost their wings;
the woods are brittle yellow.

But we go on swimming, swimming.
It is part of our love.
We give off rings of chilly waves
from one still center. Tonight
there is nothing but skin between us:
the rest is water.

Winter of the Dog

Blue winds harrow the valley,
click in the bones of willow,
snag in crab grass nesting in the dirt.

A crow is locked in the ice of heaven.

The river wants breaking.

Winter of the Dog,
Winter of the Wolf's Tooth,
Winter of the Chase.

I need your spring now, need

that country of affection:
green moons rising through a twilight
warm as skins, the tawny eucalyptus
stripped of bark, its whispered smells,
the fly-worms burning in the leaves.

This Scrying

"Thus the conditions under which the scryer can scry are, as yet, unascertained."
—ANDREW LANG

Pausing by the sink, half stooped,
I study tea leaves emptied in a drain,
the sawdust sweetness of the pulp,
the pattern of my life to come
spread out before me like a map
in darkness I cannot cut through.
I run the tap, seeing how
the conditions will elude me further,
though I stare through centuries,
blinking into spheres, or hold
my palm out, tracing
my affections in a scrawl of lines.
And whether I shall have you here
beside me for another night
I will learn by reading closely
from your lips, but you
say nothing. It would seem,
the conditions against this scrying
are a bold prevention figured in the stars.

To His Dear Friend, Bones

The arguments against restraint
in love, in retrospect, seem quaint;
I would have thought this obvious
to you, at least, whose serious
pursuit of intellectual grace
is not less equal to your taste
for all things richly formed. No good
will come of what we force. I should
be hesitant to say how long
this shy devotion has gone on,
how days beyond account have turned
to seasons as we've slowly learned
to speak a common tongue, to find
the world's erratic text defined
and stabilized. I should be vexed
to mention time at all, except
that, even as I write, a blear
October dampness feels like fear
externalized; I number days
in lots of thirty—all the ways
we have for counting breaths, so brief,
beside the measures of our grief
and joy. So let me obviate
this cold chronology and state
more simply what I mean: it's sure
enough, the grave will make obscure
whatever fierce, light moments love
affords. I should not have to prove
by metaphysical displays
of wit how numerous are the ways

in which it matters that we touch,
not merely with our hearts; so much
depends upon the skin, dear bones,
with all its various, humid tones,
the only barrier which contrives
to keep us in our separate lives.

Sleepers

When in the course of sleep you turn and touch
my shoulder, hanging on to me as if
the scalloped ocean of your dreams were much
too much to bear alone, I know the cleft
that forms between true lovers when they sleep
is partial, almost something to be wished
were it not there. And when from that same deep
a garbled syllable of fear is fished
and tossed between us on the waking deck
with cool and jeweled eyes, I wait to see
if sleep won't come again to haul it back
beneath those waters. Huddled in the lee
of our affection, we can well afford
cold creatures, distances, the alien word.

Her Sadness

He held her. She was sad.
And nothing could disguise
the mist upon her eyes.
Yet every way he spoke
seemed only to evince
the sense that something bad
had happened in her night.
The room was full of light;
it settled on the flowers
beside their bed, the sheets
illumined by the sun.
He knew of all the powers
beyond what he could see:
the current of her dreams
wherein she had been whirled,
for hours tossed and churned.
"I love you," he might say,
but she would turn aside
and bite her lip to chide;
the most he could provide
was skin against her skin
and silence like the moss
that covers with green fur
the sharpest, rasping ledge
in time. She wept alone,
an island in the creek
of all his running love.
By noon, when they had slept
an hour past her tears,
they went outside. Her fears

had blown off like a fog
from that disconsolate shore.
They walked, now hand in hand,
and nothing more was said.
It was as if the dead
had somehow been subdued,
at least until that dark
came down on her again.

After the Summer Heroes

For D.S.J.

After the summer heroes dwindle into names
on dusty gum-cards stacked in boxes
buried in the rooms we never search;

after all the Cokes, the candied apples,
cigarettes and beer consumed in haste,
converting into flesh and world to burn;

after all the sweethearts run amok
in cheap hotel rooms, giving in to fear
that no one in the end will grant them time

to prosper or endure, time out to waste
in painted nails and factories of hair,
in drive-ins or the harping wards of babes;

after every dream of glory or of grace
in smooth performance of the given task
is punctured by the dismal needle, time—

love, may we catch some fragment of a song,
a canticle of blessed and bitter hours,
a lost refrain to carry into night.

This Reaping

They are all going out around us,
popping off like lights—
the professors crumpled over desks,
the doctors with entrails hanging from their ears,
the operators dead at the end of lines.

They are all going out, shut off
at the source without warning—
the student tumbled from the bike in traffic,
the child in the cradle, choking,
the nun in the faulty subway.

And nobody knows the hour,
whether now or later, whether
neatly with a snap in the night
or, less discreetly, dragged
by a bus through busy corners.

What a business, this reaping
in private or public places
with so little sewing:
let us pray that somewhere
on sweaty beds of complete affection
there are lovers
doubling themselves in the lively dark.

Skater in Blue

The lid broke, and suddenly the child
in all her innocence was underneath
the ice in zero water, growing wild
with numbness and with fear. The child fell
so gently through the ice that none could tell
at first that she was gone. They skated on
without the backward looks that might have saved
her when she slipped, feet first, beneath the glaze.
She saw the sun distorted by the haze
of river ice, a splay of light, a lost
imperfect kingdom. Fallen out of sight,
she found a blue and simple, solid night.
It never came to her that no one knew
how far from them she'd fallen or how blue
her world had grown so quickly, at such cost.

Summer People

See them, the affectionate ones,
how they dawdle in the sun on watered lawns,
how they cast one shadow and call it love.

See the husbands playing at tennis,
shouting the scores, their smooth limbs
perfect in all proportions,

bobbing and weaving, winning or losing
weight and wives. Some knees are
bandaged to support their passion.

It is so important, they say,
knowing how to serve, not balking
when you swing, staying close to the line.

See the slender ladies with children
who look like themselves; they have married
these men with long vacations,

these summery people who know how
to do it, year after year,
how to find the time, the beautiful

houses on winking lakes, the friends
with even more luck than themselves,
the words to endear them each to another.

Black Week

I must parse the sentence of my sadness,
diagram despair.
I must break my anger into parts of speech:
the nouns of nothing I can do or say,
the verbs of ruin, participles
raging through my fevered nights.
I must find a stronger subject for my verbs,
disrupt the syntax of protracted fear.
I must place my anger in subordination,
possess the grammar of my own recovery,
find my predicate, someone gladly
to complete my transitive, hungry verbs.

Illimitable Kingdom

There is something about this room
you cannot pretend to say.
I stand by the window
where a green plane rises over towers.
It is full of silence, lifting
its nose into brilliant spaces.
Taxis throttle in the streets below,
but the room holds still;
the furniture waits at my convenience.

When the telephone rings, I let it
tremble and refuse to answer.
I cannot say why.
Alone in this wordless room,
I am grateful for the life
that will not give in, that keeps
on coming when the words are gone,
this world within world,
illimitable kingdom.

Near Aberdeen

"History broods over that part of the world like the easterly haar."
—ROBERT LOUIS STEVENSON

On a blue scarp, far out, musing
over water, standing where the salt winds
whet their blades on granite edges,
hogweeds rasping, marram grass and thistle,
I was north of Aberdeen,
alone and calling to a friend
as if the wind could carry to her heart
my words like spores, as if
by merely shouting in the air
past waters snarling in the rocks
affection could be raised, its sword
and fire, the blue flame
rising in the mist, the lifting haar.

High Gannet

I watch it breaking from a cliff,
a gannet with its white-silk wings,
chipped off, a piece of granite, swung out wide.

Through shelves of light it rises,
through the plum-ripe dawn,
its fringe of shadows, blood-bright clouds
accumulating orchids, froths of bloom.

Way up, it hangs an eye upon the world.

Cold sea bird, risen out of time
through mizzling fog to ice-blue air,
I know the journey you in flight describe:
from rock to water, water into fog,
from fog to sunlit drizzle into air—

to live forever in the air's idea,
mindless as a star,
a gannet in perpetual blue flight,
pure breath above the world.